My Midwest

Rural Writings
from the Heartland

edited by Philip Martin

Midwest Traditions, Inc.
Shorewood, Wisconsin
1998

Midwest Traditions, Inc. is a nonprofit organization working to help preserve a sense of place and tradition in American life.

For a catalog of books, write:

Midwest Traditions
3710 N. Morris Blvd.
Shorewood, Wisconsin 53211
U.S.A.
or call 1-800-736-9189

Cover artwork is a detail from an oil painting by Lavern Kammerude (1915-1989), a self-taught rural artist from Blanchardville, Wisconsin. His work is featured in the book, *Threshing Days*, with stories by Chet Garthwaite (Mt. Horeb: Wisconsin Folk Museum, 1990). Used by permission.

ISBN 1-883953-26-X

Original Softcover Edition
10 9 8 7 6 5 4 3 2 1

TABLE OF CONTENTS

TABLE OF CONTENTS (continued)

INTRODUCTION

These are true tales of rural life from America's heartland, from Ohio to Nebraska, from Minnesota to Missouri. Real memories, they are nonfiction accounts of things that actually happened. Yet they are more.

When memories are recorded, on paper or by the retelling of stories, they undergo a remarkable alchemy. Like a gilded, ornate frame placed around a simple landscape, the act of remembering brings a luster to the past, a selective spotlight that illuminates where it is cast, leaving all else in shadow.

And that is exactly why people tell stories. They are telling us what they choose to remember, and (if we listen carefully), why.

In 1995, Midwest Traditions, a small nonprofit independent press, sponsored a rural writing contest. We asked people to write down and send in personal memories that expressed what it meant to grow up on a farm in the Midwest. *My Midwest* is a selection of some of our personal favorites from the hundreds of stories submitted.

All the stories were wonderful; they shone with the glow of life fondly remembered. Like cutting into a fresh-baked berry pie, or slipping under a feather quilt on a cold winter night, many of these stories are filled with a sense of goodness almost too good to be believed. But then again, each time we bite into a piece of a well-made pie, or feel the lightness of a down comforter settle around us in the dark, or hear a well-told story, we realize that some things are really, truly good.

These stories resonate with the dignity of long traditions, with the wonder of a sense of place, with the bedrock values of family and neighborhood togetherness.

As the envelopes of stories submitted arrived in the mail, a handful each day for many, many weeks throughout the summer of 1995 and into the fall, my wife Jean and I would collect them at the post office in the small town where we lived, hop in our car, and drive together about 20 miles to our Midwest Traditions office.

Our office was located on a farm called Folklore Village, a rural folk center set in the rolling hills of southwestern Wisconsin. The landscape of that daily drive was overwhelmingly beautiful — sloping fields dotted with black-and-white Holstein cows, the green pastures dropping and undulating away on both sides of the long, high ridge which the highway follows on its way towards the Mississippi River, another 100 miles to the west.

Many of the fields of crops were arranged by the farmers' plows and planters into contoured strips of alternating alfalfa and corn. The contours were meant to slow erosion on the hilly terrain, but the sloped landscape also acted to display the beauty of the fields. We could not drive by those perfectly patterned fields without wondering: do

2

farmers see the beauty of the landscape so close to home, so common, so everyday?

Do farm families recognize the drama of the changing seasons? Do they value the richness of their family heritage, the ties to neighbors and the land?

As we pulled each story from its envelope and read aloud to each other, as our old car thrummed down the rural highway, on each and every sheet of each submission — some typed, some handwritten — the answer was there.

Yes, say these reminiscences. Yes, our lives, our stories, our histories in these places are priceless.

Taken as a whole, the stories can be seen to share some common ground that clearly was important to all of the writers.

First: Life is beautiful in its details. That was one of our criteria for making the selections for this anthology. Our favorite stories described rural life by recalling the small things that made it so remarkable. The good smells of a root cellar stocked with homemade provisions. The anticipation of waiting for Mother to open up the outbuilding called the "summer kitchen." The thoughts that went through a young boy's head as he sat on a bluff watching sheep. The aroma of newly-cut hay mixing with the first breezes of an incoming rainstorm, as Pa, true to form, coaxes everyone into "one more round" before the first shower arrived. Or the quirks of character in each farm's parade of hired men, footloose and fascinating to all farm children.

Mostly, the story are told in a traditional style: straightforward and realistic. We ended up awarding two first prizes. One went to Leona Buhlmann for her story set in the sandhills of Kansas. "My First Year of Teaching in a One-Room School" is a thoughtful, finely detailed recollection that lets us see, through the eyes of a young teacher, her impressions of what it was like to begin to teach in a country school.

The co-winner was Gladys Criss for her memories of growing up and "making do" in rural Missouri, in a time during the Depression when wealth was relative, where happiness meant getting two empty flour sacks of the same pattern to make a dress out of. Through their careful documentation, both these writers help us see the decisions and daily patterns, the joys and small triumphs of life in that earlier part of the 20th century.

Second: Our passage through life is shaped by values. Values shape people and their communities. In particular, Midwestern farm-family values, developed and nurtured in agricultural neighborhoods, had a huge impact on shaping an American way of life, at least for much of the first half of the 20th century. Values are often invisible, unspoken, too often undervalued. But these stories respect the power of values; they make them visible.

4

In those days, for instance, the word "neighbor" was not just a noun; it was also a verb. And a very active verb. You "neighbored" with the families around you. This constant interaction had its roots in needs of pioneer farm settlements, with their work-exchange rings, threshing circles, quilting and corn-husking bees, rural school and church socials, and the endless cycle of borrowed tools, equipment, cups of sugar and pie plates (you could never return a pie plate empty). These patterns of sharing — informal but unavoidable — were both necessary and enjoyed.

Other core values included a respect for elders and traditions, a strong work ethic, a sense of roots to a place. Today, in many ways, we are drawing on the "principle investment" of these core community values built up painstakingly over many years. Midwestern neighborhoods had a certain understanding: that you should put more into community life than you "withdrew" for your personal needs. Today, although we like to draw on that "bank" of accumulated values as needed, the balance is starting to run low.

As my wife and I drove each day to our country office, we delighted in these stories with their blend of small, tangible details and large, invisible values. The stories made us laugh and smile. They brought the history of rural ways into focus; they made us realize that each farmhouse we passed had a special story.

Yes, memories are both fact and fiction. These stories seldom speak —though they hint — of the hardships, the pain, the uncertainty, the suffering, the darker sides of rural life. The message is that stories are how we remember what we want to preserve. When we need to teach values to our children, we should always turn to stories like these.

Certainly stories are one of those rare treasures — like love and friendship — that grow greater the more they are given away. Although we all suffer from a reluctance to accept the clay feet of daily lives, sometimes we need to pause to recall that our lives are glorious in their small details — and in their immense wealth of values much greater than any one of us.

We should always share such stories.

Philip Martin
Midwest Traditions
1998

Dad Dug the Basement with Dynamite

by Sarah Busjohn

Spring Grove, near Juda, Wisconsin, 1940s

Otto Becker, a self-taught farmer-carpenter living near Oakley, Wisconsin, was lighting the fuse on the dynamite he had just placed under his own house. Even he wasn't sure that setting the dynamite under the portion of the old house which was to be saved was the right idea. But the soil under this part of the house was dry and hard. There was no way to get to it with the slip scraper and team of horses.

Before setting the charge, Dad had said, "You better take the kids and go to the barn. I'm going to blast the hard clay loose from under the house." With reluctance my mother gathered the kids and took us to the barn. As we stood there waiting, Dad came running to stand with us.

This was not the first time in my six short years that I'd peered from the barn wondering if our house would be there for us.

One cold evening, Dad had fired up the Round Oak stove in the living room with chunks of oak wood. Then he went to the barn to tend to chores. Soon, the stove turned red and the fire roared up the chimney. My mother yelled at me, "You go get your dad, tell him to get in here right away. We have a chimney fire!"

I hurried as fast as my short legs would carry me and let myself into the barn in front of the horse mangers. Our white horses kept munching their oats. I climbed the wooden partition, ran across the calf pen, and opened a small gate. From there, I could talk to Dad as he was feeding the pigs.

I said, "Dad, Ma said to get in the house right away, we have a chimney fire."

His answer came back, "Okay, I'm coming."

I waited for what seemed forever. And then I repeated my message, and back came his slightly agitated response, "Okay, I'm coming."

Even at this young age, I knew I must get my dad to come to the house. We lived six and one-half miles from the nearest town of Juda, and a half mile from our closest neighbor. We did not have a telephone. I knew that Dad was the only person who could save our house. Remembering the horrified look on my mother's face, I yelled, "Damnit, Dad, the house is on fire!" The only sound was the whoosh as he ran past me.

By the time I got back to the house, those four small rooms were filled with smoke. The Round Oak stove had simmered down somewhat. Dad was checking out the attic to see if there was fire there. The house had not caught fire. This messenger was never reprimanded for telling him the house was on fire.

And here I was again wondering if we would have a house. The muffled boom of the dynamite rattled the barn windows. Would our house still be there? The dust settled and then we went to see what the charge had done. The clay was now loose and we discovered a crack in the basement wall. But otherwise unscathed, the remaining portion of the house was ready to be added on to.

The year was 1940. My folks had endured the hardships of the Depression. Paying for a farm and feeding and clothing five kids had not been easy. When our four-room house became too small for seven people, Dad had decided we needed a new, bigger one. Undaunted by the staggering task ahead of him, he tackled the job.

Dad's determination and ability to work hard came at an early age. Barefooted, at the age of ten, he hired out as a farm hand during summer vacation. Building a house was a major undertaking for this man, who had not been allowed to write his eighth-grade exam. His father owned 20 acres of land, and my dad had to stay home and plow that land the day the tests were written.

After buying that small, hilly farm, he wrested his farmland from the timber. He blasted stumps and broke new ground with a breaking plow and a team of horses. He picked rocks and dug out boulders. He built fences to hold cattle and hogs. He remodeled some buildings and others he built new. He sawed wood to heat the house, planted gardens, cooked maple syrup, did his own butchering, milked cows by hand, dehorned cattle, castrated pigs, fixed his own machinery, churned butter, planted and harvested crops.

It was during this time of buying and building that he fell out of the silo. He was in great pain, but he continued with his farm work and milked his herd of cows. It was confirmed, by x-ray years later, that the fall had broken his back.

Dad died at age 92. His offspring marvel at how this five-foot, seven-inch bundle of energy accomplished all he did. The house is still there to offer mute testimony to one of his more successful tasks.

And when we get together to reminisce, someone is sure to ask, "Remember the day Dad dug the basement with dynamite?"

The Egg Fight
by Becki L. Wardyn

Custer County, near Mason City, Nebraska, 1948

The rhythmic creak ... crik, creak ...crik, creak of the old rocking chair that had belonged to my great grandfather had a hypnotic quality. I felt my eyes getting heavy and soon my little chin was resting on my chest. Hoping against hope that I had finally fallen asleep, Daddy stopped the gentle swing of the chair and peered over my tousled head to see my face. His whiskers tickled my forehead and woke me. "Rock," I commanded, and the chair resumed its creaking motion.

"Now once, long ago, when I was about your age..." he began, and I snuggled deeper into his embrace. Rocking was nearly an every-night ritual with us, and the stories of his childhood were the tools he used to lure me to sleep.

Daddy had spent his childhood on a small farm in Custer County, Nebraska. He and his two brothers were continually into one scrape or another, which caused my grandmother much worry as to whether her boys would ever reach adulthood. Daddy was the middle child, with my Uncle Denny being the oldest, and my Uncle Rod the youngest. The story my father had begun was an escapade of theirs that was a special favorite of mine, and one

I asked for night after night.

Grandma had strictly forbidden her boys from entering the henhouse for eggs. The sale of those eggs provided grocery money for the things that the farm didn't produce, so she couldn't afford to have them broken over little boys' skulls. It was never wise to disobey Grandma Hiser, even indirectly.

But Denny, Daddy, and Rod knew of every nest in every nook and cranny of the farm that just happened to be located *outside* of the henhouse. The boys even took extra precautions not to throw away good eggs by hauling their finds down to the horse tank. You see, rotten eggs float, so if the little orbs sank, the boys wouldn't use them. If they floated … ammunition.

Now, Uncle Rod was no dummy. He knew by observation that his oldest brother could throw straighter and farther than Daddy, so when it came time to choose sides, he could be found holed up in the hayloft with Uncle Denny. The barn wall was full of peepholes and cracks for the team of two to spy on their target, my father.

No matter how stealthily he sneaked or from what angle he crept, Daddy would have to bolt for cover when a barn door suddenly opened and showered rotten bombs on his little head. In fact, some of the eggs were so rotten that they would explode in mid-flight and spill their stinking contents everywhere. Obviously my daddy faced a dilemma. Yet outnumbered and outclassed though he was, he was far from being outsmarted.

The toys my daddy had back then were not of the store-bought variety. Much of what the boys played with they had invented, using bits of scrap lying around the farm. They even had a special corner of Grandpa's workshop in which they tinkered on their contraptions. It was in this shop that Daddy found the solution to his problem. An old windmill wheel had been stored there after it had blown down many months ago. One of its fan blades would make an excellent shield against egg bombs.

Using a cold chisel, Daddy began pounding away at the rivets that held the windmill blade to the wheel. When it pulled free, he then took some tin snips and cut four one-inch notches, two on each side, into the blade. These notches held in place two lengths of leather, wrapped around the blade. The straps then became handles when Daddy stuck his left arm up between the leather and metal. This left his right arm free for throwing.

Now he was set. Once again he tiptoed within range of the barn. Quietly now ... quietly. Zing! ... Zing! ... Zing! The loft door flew open with a new battery of putrid bombs. But each well-aimed egg splattered harmlessly on my father's new shield. Chuckling to himself, he wound up for the retaliation.

"You boys! I thought I told you never to steal eggs from my henhouse!" Grandma bellowed as she thundered down the hill.

Blood drained from the brothers' faces as they tried to explain. "But Mamma, we didn't get them from the henhouse. We..."

"I don't care! I don't want you throwing any of my eggs!"

"But Mamma! They're all just rotten ones! We didn't..."

"It doesn't make any difference! I told you I don't want you throwing any of my eggs!" she countered, and proceeded to beat them with the dreaded rubber spatula.

Daddy laughed at the memory. "So that was the end of our egg wars," he said and gave my body a squeeze.

When I didn't stir, he slowly stopped rocking. "Works every time," he whispered to himself, then gently lifted me from his lap and carried me to bed.

The New Stove

by Beth Richardson

near Belleville, Republic County, Kansas, 1926

This Mother's Day a new electric stove has come into our home. It has all the gadgets that the most mechanized mind could think of. It is white, big, and gorgeous, and I am happy to have it.

But the thrill of it can never compare with an event that took place when I was a big girl of eleven years old. We were a large farm family and this was during the "hard years" — we had in our farm kitchen an old black iron stove, common in those days.

My dad sold a cow and got the big price of eighty dollars for her. With a twinkle in his eyes, he told me that next morning he and I would go to Fairbury. I didn't know why. To go anywhere was a treat — even to our local town. But to go to a town fifty miles away was an unheard-of event.

Oh, it was cold that morning! As I remember it was cloudy, with a good wind. And I cringe as I remember how I was dressed — long underwear of course, black stockings, a heavy sweater, a pair of my brother's o'alls over all, and then a big Mackinaw, stocking cap, and mittens. Remember, the car was a touring car. Of course, Dad had the black curtain on, but a heater was as yet unheard of. Dad hitched the old wooden trailer on behind, and away we went. To say the least, it was a long, cold, fifty-mile trip.

At the Montgomery Ward store, we went up the stairs to the second floor. There were the stoves. Beautiful, beautiful stoves. White, blue, ivory, and black. But the newest cookstoves were porcelain, with silver on them and streamlined to the nth degree. And my beloved Dad let me pick out Mother's new stove. What a responsibility!

But let no one say that a woman of eleven didn't know just what was necessary. Every oven had to be looked into, every warming oven door opened. Each lid was lifted. My Dad stood back, letting me choose. After due deliberation, I knew the ivory one was exactly right. I don't remember them loading it up, but I do remember the price — $69.95 — a terrific price.

Believe me, I was warmer with excitement on the way home. But the trip was twice as long. I thought we'd never get home. Mother thrilled, "Oh, Owen," when she saw our stove.

I remember the beauty of that ivory stove in our kitchen where the black one had stood — the loving care with which it was wiped off after every meal. The convenience of having the reservoir of hot water at all times. The pure luxury of a brand new stove, standing there in all its glory.

16

It served us well. Mother baked bread every other day — six loaves — along with two big pans of raisin buns. And every day she baked either cake, pies, or cookies. And the big kettles of navy beans and ham, beef stew, big skillets of fried potatoes — the thought of it makes my mouth water.

Just One More Round

by Elizabeth Marquard

Lyme Township, near Bellevue, Ohio, 1960s

Haying season on the farm always seemed, I recall, to coincide with the end of the school year, when summer stretched deliciously before us. Playing in the muddy creek, looking for Indian arrowheads in the neighbor's sandy soybean field, or just lounging in the languid sway of the hammock were the only imminent activities my two brothers and I envisioned.

That is, until we spied Dad scudding across the field on his John Deere tractor with the hay rake furiously fluffing windrows behind him. As sweet as the smell of freshly-cut clover was, it smacked of work. Our youthful hearts sank as the call to bale hay came on that first day of summer vacation.

Down the driveway we lumbered. Dad drove the tractor, followed by the temperamental old baler which seemed almost as reluctant as us kids to begin another haying season. Mom, my brothers, and I pitched and swayed on the empty haywagon. Past the shade-dappled hammock, past the inviting coolness of the creek, past the impassive faces of the cud-chewing, tail-swishing cows, out into the hot open expanse of the hay field we paraded.

Mom assumed her duties at the wheel of the tractor. The cantankerous baler sputtered to life with its rhythmic grind, hum, grind, hum as it chewed up the windrows of hay and spit out neatly packaged bales to be stacked on the rocking wagon-bed by Dad, the boys, and me.

The perfect day for baling hay was one so hot and still that it seemed our only chore should be pulling air into the lungs. Around and around the field we crawled, with the blazing sun crisping our skin. Tiny pools of perspiration on our arms and necks trapped the itchy chaff blown backward from the baler, whose grinding cadence had become hypnotic.

Occasionally, the feisty old baler snorted and gasped to a stop. Dad, who could fix anything with a pocketknife, performed surgery on it while the rest of us sought brief respite from the stifling heat under the wagon. There we passed around the scuffed canteen and enjoyed a refreshing swallow of ice-cold well water.

Just when it seemed the day could get no hotter or longer, a too-cool breeze floated in from the west, and five pairs of eyes turned toward the boiling black thunderclouds marching our way. Four pairs of eyes rolled dubiously skyward, as Dad confidently ordered, "Just one more round." He didn't earn the nickname "One Round Too Many" by getting us all to the safety of the barn with dry clothes and dry hay!

And sure enough, midway through that "one more

round," when we were at the farthest corner of the hay field, the fat raindrops began to splatter with electrifying chill on our backs. We hastily unhooked the baler from the tractor, replaced it with the loaded hay wagon, and wheeled for home at a breakneck speed. The white wall of rain raced over the fields behind us and inevitably overtook us just minutes from the dry sanctuary of the barn.

We five soaked farmhands stood in the barn doorway, watching the rainfall and enveloped by the fragrance of freshly-baled hay. It was an aroma not only of hard work, but also of open fields, clean air, and a family toiling together.

Bells on Her Bridle

by Dorothy J. Fry

Peoria Township, near Peoria, Illinois, 1929-1936

"A circus horse? Out here? You what?" Mother's voice rose ten decibels. Agitated, she shot up from the kitchen chair, knocking over her glass of water, making the plates tremble.

I lowered my head a bit, like a turtle seeking the protection of its shell. A child of thirteen shouldn't have to deal with this. My eyes turned sideways to see what Pa was doing. He was still as the pyramids and as solid and unmoved.

"A year. A year is nothing. And then, back she goes."

Mother jerked her chair around to face him head-on. "Explain this to me, Howard. Tell me why we will be so privileged. Justify to me this added responsibility that I will have in addition to the garden, to the turkeys, the ducks, the cow, the pigs, the bums who stop by for a meal, the St. Bernard, the cherry orchard, the canning, plus you and two children."

Plus, I added mentally, the grand piano on which she itched to practice, the English club she attended twice a month, the fashionable clothes she stitched in the middle of the night. This 1930s Depression was Mother's archenemy and there would be no retreat ... or Pa would hear about it!

Having lost the amenities of life which were our due, we had purchased an old farm house on ten acres of hills. Purchased it with one hundred dollars, cash, and a loan from the owner of the property, if you can believe that! Our house was cupped in a meadow surrounded by wooded heights, much as if we were cupped in the palm of a giant hand. While Mother had never felt the need of a coal house or a hen house or a barn, she was now the proud owner of all she surveyed.

Pa continued, "It was exciting! The phone rang this morning at the office." (That was the small-animal hospital of which Pa was owner and veterinarian, and which we hadn't lost). "You'll never guess who it was!" He waited a suspenseful moment for Mother to become involved. She didn't.

He plunged ahead. "Ringling Brothers Circus! They wanted me to come out to the grounds immediately. Wanted me to shoot her. Anna, she was a beautiful animal. She turned her head when I came up ... looked at me, that look in her eyes..." Pa had been known to be more easily swayed by his patients than by us.

"Like this look in my eyes, Howard?" No mistaking Mother had thrown down the glove.

"Reminded me of you, Love. That's why I couldn't ... well, I just couldn't."

"You mean we're going to have a horse out here, Pa? A real circus horse? One we can ride? Oh, Pa!" The kitchen was neutral again. Children could speak. Mother had been overcome by the Irish.

Pa looked at me affectionately, and said, "We will have a wonderfully beautiful circus horse here in the field next to the barn. We won't be riding her. We'll be taking care of her because her broken leg will be set and in a cast. And, I talked them into this! I did!"

Mother interrupted, "Howard, you talked them into what? You mean the horse is not ours?"

"Ringling felt there was no option to shooting the horse. I gave them one. I felt I could set the leg so that it would be good as new. I made them a deal. I would bring Sparkle — that's her name — home, let her get well. Next year when the circus is back they can come see her — try her out. If she's able to resume her work, they will pay me the treatment bills plus board for the year. If not, then she's ours."

"Will she and Greta hit it off?" (Greta was the cow.) Mother seemed resigned now to adding a horse to our zoo.

"Should."

I flew out the screen door, jumped the three steps to the ground from the back concrete slab, and called for Bill, the St. Bernard, who came loping around the house, his tongue hanging out of his huge black muzzle. He was my best friend. I'd have to tell him about Sparkle. We trudged up the side of the hill; I held the wires of the fence up at the depression in the ground where we always went under. Bill flattened on his belly and inched through. I made it by myself.

Our "zoo," as Mother termed it, was Pa's best effort to survive. We had to move out of the city. Pa thought it was pure miracle that John Krempp (the "greenhouse Krempps") decided to sell the old home place and even loaned Pa the down-payment. Mother was outraged when she saw the sprawling Victorian farmhouse on the hill. Her shock was complete on entering the second living room to note the red-painted "Gents" on the door of the bathroom. Its interim use had been as a roadhouse.

"The interior will be painted ivory, every room. Hardwood floors will be laid so I can put my orientals down. If these things aren't done in three weeks, I will leave for Kansas City." (Mother's people lived in Kansas City.) She had spoken.

In return Pa was given leave to populate the barnyard. Already there was a peach and a cherry orchard, a long-time bed of strawberries, and a bed of asparagus. He only needed to amplify the garden with more vegetables, and to supply meat and milk. The cow, Greta, was the barn's first tenant (Mother bought a churn), quickly followed by two piglets, four turkeys, and a mother duck with a fluffy yellow trail of ducklings. This family would be able to weather the economy's death-throes. We would be self-sufficient.

To my brother and me, this was not the lifeboat keeping us afloat while the ship went down; this was a virginal, forested Happy Hunting Ground. We always contended that ours were the first feet to touch this wilderness. We were still of this mind even when we found the arrowheads.

A horse-carrier from the circus delivered Sparkle to our meadow. A strange creature she was, with a white well-muscled body — gracefully made, but with one leg in cast, a comedy of tentative errors. She poked around the inside of the fence, using the cast as a crutch, practicing with it. Greta turned tail and munched grass as far as possible from this bizarre "other cow."

In spite of all this planning, the progress, the forward movement contrived by my parents, we had a sudden reversal, a death in our midst ... the mama duck. Pa thought a weasel had gotten her. We rigged up a washtub, set it in the middle of an old tractor tire we'd found in the barn, filled it with water and then with six baby ducks. After swimming, they climbed out on the rubber tire and tumbled to the ground.

But they needed a place to snuggle down at night. We considered several sizes of box, or even an old rug ... then we put the rug in the largest box, and put that box near the back door on the concrete slab so they would be safer. That night, my brother Bob and I tucked them in and unwillingly went in the house to bed. Bill, the St. Bernard, slept out there too. He'd watch.

Brother shook me by the shoulder. I opened one eye. It was a crispy cold morning. I shot further under the quilt.

"Come on. We have to go see Sparkle," he said.

Energized by this prospect, it took me two minutes to pull on my jeans, my undershirt, and my sweater. Without untying my laces, I contorted toes and heels into my old tennis shoes. We were off!

Pa was dressing. Mother presided over a hot frying pan ... the rich brown smell of bran muffins seeping out the oven door. She was dressed. There would be no letting down even though we were stuck in this rusticity. "Hah! You two are finally up. I was just going to call you."

She motioned to the table where sat a pile of plates and silverware, napkins and glasses, and a squat vase of nasturtiums. I scrambled to get it set, putting china on the endangered list. "I did it, Mom. And please, we want to go to the fence to see Sparkle. We'll say 'hi!' and come right back."

Mother smiled. "You'll have time. I hear Pa shaving. Oh, by the by, take Bill with you. I don't know whether he's sick. I went out to get the nasturtiums and he didn't go with me. Not that I wanted him to. He's death on flowers! When I came back I rubbed his head but he didn't offer to get up, just rolled his eyes at me."

We were stopped in our tracks; the same sick thought

was reflected in Brother's eyes.

The two of us dashed out the door onto the concrete porch. Bill was lying there, his huge head resting on one outstretched paw. The box for the ducklings was empty. Our child's belief in all good things was shattered. But, Bill! Not our rescue dog with an imaginary keg around his neck. Not our friend. Miserable, we stood looking at him. He didn't budge, just rolled his eyes.

In a falsetto peculiar to nine-year-old boys with tears in their throats, Robert said, "We was going to take you with us to see Sparkle."

Mother bustled through the door. What was holding us up? She grabbed Bill by the collar. "Come on, you 'ton of food,' go with them." Bill resisted. He wouldn't even lift his head.

Brother saw it first. "Oh, Mother, don't step! It's a baby duck! There! There's another one!" Little heads were popping out all round the long fur. Bill was their nest! He was their mama. When the ducklings were out and had walked away, Bill got to his feet.

We survived the winter though it seemed it would never end. Pa was shoveling coal into the hopper in the earthen cellar almost faster than we could buy it. No attempt was made to heat the upstairs where the bedrooms were, but we congregated by the big stove in the kitchen to dress for the day. It had a wood-burning section. Privacy was achieved only by the spacing of arrival times.

Winter, almost over, was now a transparent glaze of ice on the ground in the morning. Tight-fisted brown buds accented the tree limbs. There seemed to be more birds, more air, more light.

Sparkle had her cast off. Such a showman ... the way she lifted her hooves, the way she held her head, ears up, and her tail a white cascade. And through the winter, being approximately the same size as Greta, the two had formed a clique, undeniably superior to the rest of the barnyard stock. They also had a routine. Sparkle had trained Greta to walk a large circle in the field as though they were in the ring. We'd sit at the table, look out the kitchen window, and see the two of them, performing.

We sat thus one Sunday morning enjoying the spectacle.

Pa looked sternly at Brother, "I've a feeling you aren't latching the barn door at night. Otherwise, they couldn't be out in the field, could they?"

Bob and I burst into laughter, stumbling all over our words to explain. We'd been waiting for the big revelation to come. Bob choked, "Pa, Sparkle don't need us to open that barn door. She does it herself ... like nothin' ... just flips it up with her nose and pushes a little. Me and Sister —" Mother interrupted with "Sister and I" to which he bobbed his head. "Sister and me put her in the barn yesterday. Then we hid up in the loft. Finally, she just walked over to that door, opened it as easy as anything. She lets Greta out too."

Our meals by that window were in the nature of ringside seats from which we watched and analyzed the barnyard stock. Pa used it as a sort of "animal primer of behavior disorders." From our window on the world, we diagnosed Stubby and Tubby, the pigs, as neurotic. They seemed normal enough when alone, rooting around in the dirt, sensually lolling in mud puddles. It was in the uninvited confrontations with the turkey hens that their pig world fell apart.

The hens were all "Mrs." — widows, I presume. The family had spent a creative Sunday breakfast providing names for the turkeys: Mrs. Peabody, Mrs. Beakon Hill (Pa's contribution since he was the only one who'd been anyplace), Mrs. Pratt, and Lola. Aggressive personalities, all. The four girls.

Pa said we could learn a lot from the animals. Stubby and Tubby were heavier than "the girls," but they "thought small." On the other hand, "the girls" were conceited; arrogance would separate them from all the richness of friendship.

"But the greatest lesson of all," Pa said, "is that Sparkle made Greta believe she's a circus queen ... and maybe she is."

There was, all at once, a lot of subterranean dialogue between Mother and Pa. They'd hush in mid-sentence if I walked in. It had to be about money. But one day I was curled on the couch in the front living room, reading, when I heard them talking in the next room.

Mother said, "It's such a big fee. You think she's old enough?"

Pa replied, "Old enough ... and in heat. It's time, Mother. Just as you said, all our money seems to be going out. The business is supporting the livestock. They're bringing nothing in. But of course, that isn't really true. We will eat them in the end." Mother shuddered in distaste. "Greta is supplying milk and butter. She could also supply a calf."

"But, the fee?"

"I have an unforeseen source of revenue. We are the ... uh, beneficiaries of a stroke of luck in the 'oldest profession.'" (They lost me right there. I couldn't imagine what the oldest profession could be unless it was teachers.) "These ladies have been bringing their poodles in for shots, for everything, and have promised that next week after the Shriners' convention, they'll be in to pay the bill. Appropriate, don't you think?" A lot of laughter.

A truck was borrowed. A neighbor came to help Pa load Greta for the trip. She and Pa left early one morning. Bob was building a tree house out front. Mother was playing the piano.

I decided to go for a hike with Bill before lunch. I barged through the screen door, Bill's signal to come running. Not a sound. No Bill. I walked around the house. No Bill. Oh, maybe the barn. I kicked a stream of pebbles up the drive all the way to the barn. I saw Stubby and Tubby rooting under an old wagon. "The girls" were primly pursuing a trail of corn that had leaked from a sack as it was carried to the barn. The ducklings were having a dip in the washtub. Who wasn't accounted for?

Bill wasn't there. And Greta was on her way to her "affair." I had finally tumbled to the thing that was going on.

The odd thing was, Sparkle wasn't anywhere to be seen either. But, she should be in the field, and the field was fenced. Sure, she could open the door to the barn. But there was no door to the fence. I stumbled, dimwittedly, around the inside of the fence. Then I saw it. The wires were all caved in to the ground, like something heavy had sat on it.

Sparkle had sat on it. "Mother," I screamed.

Ten minutes later, Mother, Bob (in the rumble seat), and I had reached the highway along the river. We were mute with worry for fear the horse had chosen this way to come. Cars would be a terrible hazard to Sparkle.

Mother's eyes, as she drove, were intent on the road as being the main danger. My eyes wandered the landscape. They finally fell on a young man, bridle in hand, leading Sparkle in our direction. Trotting alongside was Bill. He and Sparkle were definitely on holiday. The boy was a Krempp. Krempps had moved their greenhouse to the highway where it would have more exposure. Mother pulled the car off the road beside the threesome.

Young John said, "I spotted these two from the greenhouse. I stepped out and whistled, then I called them by name." He laughed. "They come when you call 'em. Why don't I just lead her on home. You can drive the kids, Ma'am." Bob jumped out to walk with them.

Pa drove in about sundown, he and Greta. We opened the door to the barn. The fence wasn't yet fixed. Oh, did we have a lot to tell him! We kept interrupting each other but he got the jist.

He looked at us, tiredly. "I think you're right. I think Sparkle set out to find Greta, and Bill just went along."

We walked with Pa to the house. Supper was almost ready, and we were a hungry lot. Mother caught Pa's eye. "How did she do?"

Pa looked at us and said, "We went to Martin's farm to breed Greta to a bull ... so she'd have a calf." He stopped.

Mother said, impatiently, "And, how did she do?"

"She didn't. Oh, she was in heat all right. The bull thought she was a knockout." He smiled at us. "I was kind of proud of Greta ... she's discriminating. She just kept moving out of the way and looking daggers at him. Be-

32

sides, she thinks she's a circus queen."

All this backward glance is the re-run of an old film where each person, each event is highlighted, projected to the foreground in heroic size from the black backdrop of the Depression. My upward gaze, as a child, was circumscribed by the form of those persons I loved: my parents. My world was ten acres of secrets in underbrush, clouds caught in trees, the wonderful coal house full of pretends, our extended family of disturbed pigs, and hens with hubris, of Bill and Greta and Sparkle. My world was serene. Up there, where my folks stood, storms broke over their heads in a fury lasting for years.

So Brother and I were rapturous children of the Depression. Our years of smelling the strawberries made an imprint on our souls that is as identifiable in adult life as a fingerprint.

Pa was no husbandryman even with his profession. He was wrong to stock the farm in order to eat the stock. We ate not a single one. It is humbling to tell you that, number one, Stubby and Tubby outgrew us. They had to be sold. Secondly, the rest of the barnyard flock lived out their life-span, entertaining and instructing us.

Spring, a year after Sparkle joined us, saw Ringling Brothers pull a horse-trailer into the lot. Pa was out there with the men and Sparkle. We all stayed in the house. This was my first yearning after a wish I knew wouldn't be.

Our Hired Men

by Julianne J. Johnson

Swede Grove Township, near Grove City, Minnesota, 1960-1975

Like hobos and gypsies, the hired men that lived and worked on our farm are long gone and far removed from my world today. But the memories of men like Maureenus, Ed, Russell, and Floyd, to name a few, are rich and humorous and always conjure a mental picture as varied as a patchwork quilt.

Characters they were; full to the brim with stories greatly embellished and tales of places we kids could only dream about. I guess I knew better, but I was utterly fascinated by them, footloose and unbound by rules of tradition. If they felt like working, they stayed; if not, they jumped into their rusty old cars and barreled down the road, clouds of dust surrounding their departure. "Guess he's had enough," Dad would inform us, and we knew the search was on for the next untethered soul who could assist with the impending marathon of harvesting grain or putting up hay.

I can still hear their laughter ringing out over one of Dad's jokes, see the swirl of acrid smoke from the butt of a filterless Lucky Strike, but more than anything, I can smell their sweaty bodies, earthy and unwashed in my mother's tidy kitchen.

In spite of their common traits like old overalls, tobacco-stained fingers, and bathlessness, their unique personalities make them easily remembered as individuals.

Maureenus, with red hair — and a face and temper to match — wasn't with us for very long. "Whattaya staring at? Ain'tcha got any work to do?" he'd fire out at us kids and we'd scatter immediately. After a few weeks, he never came back.

"Just can't work with a man that owly," Dad calmly remarked as he sipped his coffee. "We'll find someone else."

When Ed lumbered on the scene, we soon found ourselves with more broken equipment than we could imagine. He was careless and sloppy but jolly as Santa Claus. He was a refreshing change from Maureenus, but Dad just couldn't get him to finish a job. He'd take long smoke breaks and spend time with us kids.

He told us lots of harmless tales of adventure, but he also taught just a few too many new words. When my little brother slipped in some profanity over the scrambled eggs one morning, Mother got the bar of soap and we were strongly admonished by Dad, "Stay away from Ed. We've got work to do and so do you."

Before long, Ed too was leaving. "Just can't work with a guy that rammy," Dad mused as Ed rattled off down the drive.

Next on the scene was Russell, lean and bronzed, with a shock of gray hair and a long Roman nose. He called himself a "half-breed" and he was very proud of his heritage. We were in awe of Russell; he was strong and tireless and worked a job till it was done. He was a wonder to watch. Sinewy and lightning-quick, he could climb a silo or dig a ditch but he hardly spoke a word.

Dad didn't care. He thought he'd died and gone to heaven, working with Russell at his side. But one day, after a couple of months, Russell got the urge to move on. He gathered his things, grabbed his check, and headed out.

Dad, not one to lose sleep over small matters, explained his nonchalance this way, "It *is* hard to work with a guy that doesn't talk."

Once again the search was on for a new man. Just how we happened upon Floyd escapes me, but he was the last hired man we ever had. He was tall and thin, with wild salt-and-pepper hair. He had brown squinty eyes, no top teeth, and a permanent grin that made him resemble a good-natured chimpanzee.

He was verbose and loved to tell stories, and was always somewhat surprised when we didn't believe half of them. My dad, who had a nickname for everyone, called Floyd "Ford" or "V-8," as he incessantly made engine noises when he wasn't talking.

Floyd loved our family and found a niche right away.

36

He was always a bit vague about his past, so we weren't sure where we went when he wasn't with us. But he loved to tell of his days in the service and about all the action he'd seen in battle. He seemed too old for World War II and too young for World War I, but we never dared question him too much. We felt he'd be hurt if we didn't take him seriously.

Floyd would come and go. Sometimes when he was gone for several months, we were sure that he'd never come back. But year after year, he faithfully returned to our farm at just the right moment. About the time Dad thought he should be looking for an extra guy to help out, there'd be Floyd, striding down our road with his little black suitcase in tow.

"Well look at that," Dad would say with a wide grin. "Just in time to help with the haying."

Floyd slept in our basement on a small cot in the corner. One particularly cold fall night, my mother felt sorry for him sleeping in a chilly basement and tiptoed down with an extra blanket. Dad always loved to tease her after that about the night she brought Floyd a quilt and never came back. Of course, knowing Mother's chaste behavior, Floyd's fear of women, and Dad's love of a joke, we weren't at all disturbed by the story.

Once my brothers were old enough to take the place of a hired man, we needed Floyd less and less. He was getting older and said he'd like to retire and move closer to some cousins he had several miles away. Shortly after that, we got the news that Floyd had died.

One day last spring, while cleaning out the garage, we came across a sketch Floyd had made of a tractor. Down to the last detail, it was perfectly drawn. None of us had ever seen him hold a pencil, much less viewed him as an artist. It was a talent we never knew he possessed.

But finding that sketch after twenty-five years was like a gift — a gentle reminder of the immense creative power that lies within each of us, from the greatest to the simplest of men.

A Rural 1920s Christmas

by Marie G. Baumgartner

Milwaukee Township, Wisconsin, 1920s

Christmas in rural Wisconsin in the 1920s lives in my memory as an exciting magical season.

It began shortly after Thanksgiving, when our small St. John's Lutheran School began to practice singing German and English Christmas carols. Preparing for the Christmas Eve program at our church next door was the highlight of the winter. Speaking "pieces" were eagerly memorized and practiced both at school and with our parents at home. We did not want to be embarrassed by needing to be prompted as we performed in front of all our parents, neighbors, and friends crowding the little rural church.

To add to the excitement of those weeks preceding Christmas, we were treated to a visit from Santa in his sleigh, with his helper, "Billy the Brownie," at his side. Schusters, a department store on the north side of Milwaukee, sent this unbelievable surprise out on a flatbed truck to our little country school. Our entire enrollment gathered around this awesome guest in wonderment. Each of us received a small coloring book about Billy the Brownie's adventures. How we treasured that gift!

A small notice was included which stated that if our parents brought us to the store in town to see Santa and his live reindeer, we could get a larger gift for just a quarter. Many parents were persuaded to make that trip ... including mine.

After weeks of practicing songs and recitations, it was time for the presentation. School was not in session in the afternoon so mothers had a chance to get children ready in their Sunday best. My mother often put my hair in rag curls and tried to get me to take a nap. I don't remember either project being very successful. After supper, Mom, my brother, and I got bundled up for the half-mile walk to the church. I'm sure it was not always under a starry sky, but I do remember it that way.

We kids in our finery gathered in the church basement all a'twitter. Finally it was time to find our preassigned partners and march up the stairs and down the center church aisle, singing "Ihr Kinderlein Kommet," the German version of "Oh Come All Ye Children." We felt so proud and important ... and excited. The program usually went off quite well and any little mistakes were generously overlooked or forgiven by doting parents and friends.

When it was over, the school board handed out brown paper bags of treats. Each one contained a popcorn ball, some hard candy, an orange, and some unshelled nuts. We really looked forward to those treats.

More excitement was to come. Now we would quickly

go home to see if Santa had come to our house while we were away. As we hurried along the highway, we talked with other families also on their way home ... all anxious to find Santa surprises.

From a distance, my brother and I could see lights of a Christmas tree in our front window. Mom could hardly keep up with us as we raced to our door. Santa had brought a Christmas tree. What other gifts would we find? Unbundling ourselves, even before we got inside, we raced to the parlor.

There was our tree, complete with lighted candles clipped to its branches with small metal clips. Under it lay white tissue wrapped gifts, tied with red and green string. Some of it was interwoven with gold or silver threads. Inside those packages we found games, toys, books, and new mittens. Sometimes a sled or skates lay there too. One time, a small black cocker-spaniel puppy slept in a basket under the tree. We could not have been happier.

It was great that our dad could be there to help Santa get all this ready for us. We always thought Dad never went to see our program because, as a florist, he was so exhausted from his busiest time of the year.

We tried out our new games and then had hot cocoa and some of our mother's good homemade Christmas cookies before bedtime.

Christmas Day was a day to enjoy our new gifts and then walk down the road to have Christmas dinner with our uncles, aunts, and cousins ... and to compare notes on what Santa had brought. The adults, too, visited until well into the evening.

I can clearly recall my father carrying a very tired daughter on his shoulder as we walked under the starry sky and heard the power lines "singing" in the cold clear night.

The memories of those Christmases of my childhood in the twenties are warm and pleasant.

The Summer Kitchen

by Grace E. Rupert

Fairfield Township, near New Waterford, Ohio, 1923

"How soon can we move out to the summer kitchen?"

"Oh, I have no idea. I don't even have my spring house-cleaning done yet."

I had been asking my mother this same question for days. Ever since school was out and I had turned ten years of age, I was looking forward to moving out to our summer kitchen as we did every summer. This was a building separated from our house only by a walk-way.

We kids loved this building as it was a perfect place to play our favorite outdoor game, "Andy-Over." It was great to play when our cousins or friends came to visit. To play, an equal number of players lined up on each side of the building. One player threw the ball over, yelling "Andy Over!" A player catching it ran with it to the other side yelling, "Halt!" He tried to hit someone with the ball and, if hit, that person had to go over to the other side. The side ending up with the most players won. Our father and uncles liked to play too.

This building, the summer kitchen, was just one room with two cupboards, a coal range, two windows, and an old dining table with chairs. This was before electricity and indoor plumbing, so there was no running water or a sink.

Finally, one day, I saw my mother scrubbing the cupboards in the summer kitchen. Excitedly, I asked, "Can we move out tomorrow?"

"No, I have to wash tomorrow."

Then I knew the day after that would be ironing day, so there went our moving. Sometimes I found myself thinking that we'd never move out. Just when I had given up, I saw my mother washing the walls and the floor of the summer kitchen. Then my sisters washed the windows till they shone and put pretty curtains on them. I tried to help but my two older sisters said I was in their way. But I was allowed to wash the table and chairs.

"Now can we move out tomorrow?" I asked.

My mother said, "We'll see."

I ran around the house, I was so happy. "We'll see," in my mother's language, meant yes.

That evening I saw my sisters carrying pots, pans, and dishes to the summer kitchen. I nearly jumped out of my skin. Good, I knew we'd move out the next morning. They couldn't cook in the house without pots and pans.

Hurrah! It was hard to go to sleep. Tomorrow we'd be eating breakfast in the summer kitchen! At last!

Everybody was up early that first morning, so there was lots of help to get the old coal range hot and the table set for the family. Breakfast would taste better, I was sure.

My mother fried ham and eggs, and sliced homemade bread for toast. Our old tin toaster had a square base with four cone-shaped sides. It was placed over a hot hole where a stove lid would fit. It was my job to see that the toast did not burn. I had to turn each piece by hand so that each side was nice and brown. Then the toasted bread was kept warm by putting it up in the warming closet where the chimney gave off heat. Homemade butter was on the table for each to spread his own.

This first morning was cool, so the big wooden door was shut. Toy, our faithful shepherd dog, lay by the stove, and Tom, my cat, lay on the rocker where I had left him.

By mid-morning, the room became too warm so we opened the door. My father had made a screen door to be used when the weather became hot. It was really a pleasant place to work and live during the day or evening. Oil lamps were used when needed.

Then it was time to wash the first meal of dirty dishes. We used two dishpans — one for washing and one for rinsing. And I tried to get out of drying the dishes but I was not that lucky. I hated it. With no sink, we carried the dirty water out to throw on the garden.

It was also my responsibility to keep fresh, cool water for drinking and cooking whenever needed. This water came from a pump that was across the road from our house, so it was quite a chore for a ten-year-old. If I could have carried a full bucket like my father did, I wouldn't have had to make so many trips. He often felt sorry for me and would fill the bucket to the brim and carry it for me. And, of course, we used a dipper to drink.

Water for washing and cleaning came from a cistern that caught rain water from the house roof. We also had two big rain-barrels to catch rain water from the summer kitchen and barn roofs. A wash basin was on a bench on the back porch, and a roller towel was nearby.

After the breakfast dishes were done, it was fun to go back in the house. It was quiet, clean, and cool. Seemed like no one lived there. No one did, except to sleep! I loved it this way. I wished it would go on like this forever.

My mother never seemed to care about dirty feet or shoes trodding into the summer kitchen, but just try to sneak into the house and she'd "nail" you every time. One of my bitter memories was washing my dirty feet in the old basin on the back step. Oh, how I hated that chore, but I was always surprised at how dirty the water became. That basin was my enemy.

Our dog, Toy, considered the summer kitchen his home, but he didn't seem to mind that we moved in with him. He could open the screen door so he could come and go as he pleased. He was only allowed in the house in extremely cold weather or when a storm was brewing. He was terrified of storms. He must have thought we were loony to move in with him.

My mother did all her food preparation out in the summer kitchen. If we had company for a meal, they were entertained there, too. A lot of our neighbors had summer kitchens. And if they didn't, we felt sorry for them.

Why did families have summer kitchens? I think the main reason was to keep the dust, grime, summer heat, and mud out of their homes. Anyway, this trend continued until electricity brought vacuum cleaners and modern conveniences.

Of course, by the fall of the year, I was asking, "Can we move back into the house tomorrow?"

The Magnificent Gasper

by Bob Barnard

near Gillett Grove, Iowa, 1932

In 1932 the Depression was showing its ugly face. People were out of work in the cities and even people who were working drew low wages. It was a scary situation for the couples with families to rear. There were four of us kids then.

I was twelve years old and growing up on a small farm east of Gillett Grove, Iowa, a busy little town with two grain elevators, a lumber yard, and a grocery store that could have been called an emporium since they had so many different kinds of merchandise. They bought cream and eggs too.

Also, the town had a tavern for spirits and pool. We had a hardware store, and two garages that sold gas. There was a livestock buyer, a Milwaukee depot, an over-the-road truck line, a blacksmith, and a small bank that looked out over a small lumber yard. The school contributed to much of what went on, too. The town was the hub of my life.

In late fall, we always had several cold nights, reminding us that soon, long ghost-like sheets of blowing snow would be whipping around the buildings, bringing with it sharp dips in the thermometer.

Dad was getting ready to fill silo. Our neighbor had a silage cutter that he had sold Dad an interest in, giving us priority to be second on the run. The neighbor and Dad had set the cutter against our silo. The long pipe had a sharp gooseneck turn, and from it hung loose-fitting pipes that reached inside to the bottom of the silo, where the chopped silage flowed and later fermented, turning into perfect cattle feed.

The hired man Dad had planned to hire couldn't make it. He had taken a job some other place and wouldn't be available for a week. Dad was desperate. Mother called people in Spencer, the nearby county seat. Long distance calls to Spencer cost ten cents for three minutes, so Mother didn't make many. Our telephone office was in our little town and was a no-charge call, so she also called the bank and the tavern and grocery store.

Soon the word was out that we needed a man to help us fill silo. In our community, my dear mother was known as a super homemaker, a neat housekeeper, and a great cook. All of this would help if a prospective man should ask — and some hired men would.

For this strenuous work, pay was a dollar a day and one meal, unless you helped also with the chores. Then you got more meals. Other silos in the community were being filled too, and these part-time jobs were available for several weeks.

It was very hard work. The corn-binder bound the corn with heavy twine into bundles that would weigh about fifteen or twenty pounds, and sometime got as heavy as forty pounds. The right side of the hay-rack was removed because of the weight of the corn bundles, and we all unloaded them into the cutter the same way. With one side off, the floor of the rack was as high as you pitched the load.

The cutter was small, but it took lots of power to turn the large fan with knives, spaced to cut the corn or green grasses, alfalfa, clover, cane, and other materials into short pieces. The machine had a continuous apron that moved, carrying the bundles into the knives, and the spin of the fan blew the chopped pieces up the pipe and down the loose pipe into the silo. There, a man directed the flow, trying to pack it tight to keep the air out so it wouldn't spoil. The airtight storage with the sugars and acids preserved it.

The phone rang late the afternoon before the scheduled start of our silo-filling day. The banker told Mother a man was in town and needed a job. He volunteered to bring him out as soon as he closed the bank, if the job was still open. The banker dropped him at the barn where he saw Dad and some of the neighbors putting the silage cutter together.

Mother saw the banker drop the hired man off and she came out to the barn. The man had hitched a ride in the freight train from Webb, the small town south of Gillett Grove, but in the process lost his suitcase with all the clothes he owned.

At a glance, Mother could see he had not shaved for several days, and black perspiration lines followed the contour of his neck. Grimy, greasy smudges showed on his shirt, and his hat was also filthy. His pants were clean. He said that someone had given them to him. They were a size too big but clean. The blue shirt that every farmer wore under their seventy-nine-cent bib overalls was sweat-streaked. With the wind in the right direction, it was hard not to grimace.

Mother questioned him about where he was from, and then told him she would get him a new shirt in town. Mother left the interview, knowing kindly Dad would hire him. She picked up her purse, got into our brown Model-A Ford and headed for town since she had other groceries to buy too.

At suppertime, dear Mother met him at the door with a brand-new blue shirt — cost, thirty-nine cents. He was painfully shy but grateful. She pointed to the basement for him to change and indicated the basin of warm water on the table was for him to take a sponge bath.

She said, "Nobody eats at my table with a dirty shirt like that. I'll wash and dry it for you tomorrow."

His eyes flashed and so did Mom's. He was, it seemed, maybe two or three heartbeats away from heading down the road without supper. Then, he saw the roast chicken and gravy on the stove. His eyes softened and he went to the basement and cleaned up. At suppertime, there was little talk.

He had bummed a roll-your-own cigarette from one of the guys and saved half of it for an after-dinner smoke. As Mother showed him where he was to sleep, he lighted it casually.

As I mentioned, it was 1932. Gas at the gas station was sixteen cents a gallon. Corn was nine cents per bushel. When Mother went to town, she had tobacco on her list: two cans of Prince Albert for twenty-five cents. When she saw that he had to smoke a butt, she gave one can to him to smooth over any hard feelings.

It was his first can of Prince Albert smoking tobacco. He took it out of the brown-paper sack Mother had handed him with great delight. The British Prince Albert, dressed in the elite garb of an aristocrat, caused the most grateful smile as he fondled the full can of the sweet-smelling tobacco. He said he had always smoked but had to smoke butts, or just poor sacked tobacco. He couldn't remember when he had rolled a fresh cigarette from his own tobacco can.

He was our new hired man and down on his luck. He had been broke and out of work for weeks. Dear Mother couldn't stand the smell of Bull Durham or Stud tobacco. This was the real reason she gave him the tobacco, the same as Dad smoked. She always got two cans. For a regular customer, the grocery man would throw in the papers because most smokers rolled their own.

He turned the face of the can toward him and flipped the top back. He held it to his nose and drew a deep breath. He tore away the oil wrapping paper from the top of the can, and the sweet aroma of fresh leaf-tobacco filled the room. It was something I had never really watched closely before. Here was someone rolling his own cigarette with so much deliberation, just for a smelly old roll-your-own. Dad smoked too, but never did it with all this fanfare.

The moist, cut leaves easily conformed to the crease that his nimble finger had put in the shiny cigarette paper. He twisted the glossy, gummed-edged cigarette paper around the tobacco to form a hump-backed "gasper." He seemed hypnotized as he fumbled for a match. Thinking quickly, Betty, my fourteen-year-old sister, ran for the kitchen. Mother gave her a match so he could light his creation and we all could enjoy the sweet aroma of the Prince Albert roll-your-own.

Captivated by his deliberate actions, we watched as he drew the white tobacco smoke into his lungs for what seemed an extra long time, and exhaled with great enjoyment. Being out of work and hungry for so long had made him forget one of the things in life that some men valued as part of manhood. Carrying a "smoke" between two fingers, and "dragging" smoke into his lungs and talking through the smoke, was high on his list. Letting the "fag" hang grotesquely at the corner of his mouth with a long ash was a credit also. Having watching the way he had "scooped" his food into his mouth at supper, we all wondered when he had last sat down to a full meal, and after meals, had enjoyed the luxury of a cigarette.

He stayed with us until the silos were full throughout the run. Each night that he stayed, just before bedtime, his ritual was to light up his gasper quietly, in a spell of ecstasy, smoking it until the fire bloomed against his fingers and he awakened to reality.

Growing Up in Missouri
by Gladys M. Criss

Texas County, near Houston, Missouri, 1935-1945

In modern times I live by my calendar. The "to do" list determines what gets done. Sometimes I yearn for the simpler life, when there were fewer demands on my time, no meetings to attend, no power outages. Is the grass really greener on the other side of the fence? Was it easier, or less work, when I was growing up back on the farm?

Before we go back, let me first add the detergent and bleach and turn on the washer, and start the dishwasher running.

Take washday, for example. Today, I never designate a day for doing laundry; whenever there's a washer load of either whites or colors, I fill the automatic washing machine, put in some detergent, bleach, and fabric softener, and push the button to start. Sometimes this is done as I'm leaving the house headed to the grocery store.

When I return in about thirty minutes, I switch the clothes from the washer to the dryer, set it on "Perma Press," and again push a button to start. By taking the shirts and dresses out and hanging them up when the dryer first shuts off, there are no wrinkles and I almost never iron anything ... maybe only to put a crease in a pair of pants.

Sixty years ago, when I was growing up, things were different. Washday wasn't necessarily on Monday, though it did consume the entire day, whichever day was chosen.

First, a fire was built out in the chicken yard, and many buckets of water were pumped and carried to fill the big oval black kettle. While the water was heating, the dirty clothes were sorted into piles: the whites, the colors, and the men's dark work clothes. The two big round washtubs were set up on a sturdy bench on the screened-in back porch — one tub with warm soapy water and the other one for rinsing. The same scrub-board was used year after year; I can't remember ever getting a new one.

After soaking awhile, a dishtowel, shirt, or sock would be spread out on the washboard, a bar of lye soap rubbed over the article, then the scrubbing on the board would begin. When well scrubbed, each item would be wrung out by hand and the white things put into the black kettle of boiling water, which had a bar of lye soap cut up into it.

After boiling for about twenty minutes, the clothes were taken out of the hot water with a clean, round stick used just for this purpose. The clothes were then carried to the tub of cold water and rinsed. The second tub of rinse water would have a few drops of bluing added. This was considered a whitening agent, and some of the gray-haired womenfolk also used this in their rinse water when they washed their hair.

After this, many of our shirts, dresses, and aprons were starched before going on the clothesline to dry. Starch was made by mixing flour and cold water into a paste, then pouring in boiling water to the right consistency.

There were lots of clothes to be washed on washday, and always just once a week. We never seemed to have enough clothespins or clothesline space, so the yard fence was also used to spread clothes over, and sometimes even the shrubbery, especially for the men's overalls.

After the last of the clothes were washed and rinsed, the soapy water was used to scrub the floor on the back porch. Then the tubs were rinsed and hung on a nail to dry outside the cellar house.

On a hot summer day in Missouri, the first of the wash would be dry by noon, and often that line space was needed for additional clothes being washed. Sheets smelled fresh as they were folded neatly and carried back into the house, sometimes being put right back on the bed they had been stripped from. Clothes that had been starched were sprinkled (or dampened) and rolled up for later ironing.

Some folks had a fancy shaker (a sprinkler-type cover for a bottle) but we had no extra money for fancy gadgets, so our sprinkling was done by dipping one's hand into a dish of water and slowly distributing some water throughout the garment. We would have a basketful of clothes dampened, ready for ironing the next day.

I never used a fold-up (or store-bought) ironing board until I was married. A long, strong wide board, which was shaped more narrow at one end, was padded first with a worn-out blanket, then covered with a well-used sheet. This was placed between the kitchen cabinet and a tall chair so that the narrow end could easily accommodate a dress or pullover shirt.

We had three flat-irons, which were heated on the woodstove. When quite hot, the removable handle was clipped onto one and this iron would be used until it cooled to the point of not doing the job well. We would rotate the three irons until the ironing was completed. The iron could be tested for the correct heat by first placing a finger to the tongue, then briefly touching the hot iron.

Even though woodstoves have no control knobs to adjust the temperature, one soon learned to sense the degree of heat, whether baking a cake, boiling potatoes, or making apple-butter. Many old-time cooks will testify that their familiar woodstoves baked bread, cookies, or cake better than today's fancy gas or electric models.

Doing dishes was as much a social activity, especially following a big Sunday dinner, as it was a necessary chore. Today I merely rinse the worst of the food off the dishes and stack them in the automatic dishwasher. My main fear is not having enough room for all the pans, thus having to wash them by hand.

Back then, we put the large tea-kettle on the stove to heat the water (or used warm water from the reservoir, which is a container for water attached to the right side of the woodstove). The table was cleared, and dishes scraped.

Any milk, butter, or other food that could spoil was taken to the cellar, which was always cool. Any food scraps were fed to the dog, cats, or chickens; nothing was wasted. Peelings of fruit or vegetables were fed to the pigs, as were any weeds from the garden. Cats stayed at the barn to catch any mice that might be there. Mom always said she'd feed them only milk and bread; they had to catch their own meat, and they did.

We used two dishpans for doing dishes: one for soapy water and one for rinsing. With a large family we usually had one person washing the dishes and one drying. There was a rule in our family that worked in the dish-dryer's favor: "If you catch up, you're done." When washing, I would always keep a few pieces of silverware in my dishwater to slip into the rinse water at a moment's notice while I was busy scouring a pan, which was sometimes a lengthy chore.

Our dishtowels were made from flour sacks, bleached white, with embroidered designs in the corner. I still feel they made better dishtowels than any on the market today.

Today I wouldn't think of going shopping without a couple of twenty-dollar bills in my wallet plus my check-book, but I remember the days when I shopped very carefully with only a dime or quarter. When I was about twelve years old, I went to a fair, called the "Ol' Settlers' Reunion," with some neighbors and my dad gave me a quarter to spend. I'd never had that much money before and guarded it ever so carefully.

The sights and smells of the fairground intrigued me all day long. I ate my sack lunch, along with my friends, at noontime. On our walk back to the car in town, we passed the general store where my neighbors did their weekly grocery shopping. I looked over the dry-goods counter and picked out a pretty blue print with pink flowers. It cost ten cents a yard, and I needed two yards for a dress; that left a nickel for a big spool of thread. No tax was charged in those days.

I went home and made myself a Sunday dress with my big purchase of a quarter.

Most of my dresses were made from feed sacks. When Mama ordered chicken feed to be delivered on the milk truck run, she always requested two 100-pound bags, which guaranteed us of getting two printed feed sacks that were alike. A small person could get a dress out of two sacks, but a larger person required three. Sometimes we needed to save up to make something requiring more material, like curtains or bedspreads.

The women attended an Extension Club meeting one Wednesday each month (sometimes quilting for the hostess, or hearing a speaker from the County Extension office) and would take along any sacks to trade. Everyone benefited from this exchange, and each woman and girl in the community wore her new dress with pride.

Feed for the cows and hogs came in white unbleached bags, which were used to make sheets, mattress covers, dishtowels, underclothes ... whatever was needed.

Money, needless to say, was scarce and we made do with what we had. Clothes were worn out or handed on to someone else who could use it. Sometimes good scraps from dresses were used for quilt pieces.

I had no "boughten" dress (meaning store-bought) until I was eleven years old. Cecil, my older brother, married a well-to-do girl in Utah, and for their first Christmas sent home a beautiful box of gifts that she, no doubt, had picked out. I received two store-bought dresses, probably priced at no more than one dollar each, but in my eyes they were the most beautiful dresses I'd ever laid eyes on!

Even during my teen years I had only hand-me-downs or homemade clothing, but I wore them proudly.

The wages for farm labor were one dollar a day. We raised most vegetables and fruits, and butchered one yearling calf and two hogs each winter, plus all the chickens we needed. We baked bread and any other form of pastry or dessert. Few groceries were purchased.

Every family was like us, working hard to make ends meet, never wasting, never wanting. We saved the waxed paper that came inside cereal boxes to wrap sandwiches for school lunchboxes.

Our chief cereals consisted of cornmeal mush, oatmeal (which often had lumps), and cornflakes. It was a treat to have "boughten" bread. If our supply of light bread ran out, we sometimes took biscuits in our lunchpail. The pail itself was a five-pound lard bucket.

During this time of year, as I gather in a meager bowl of string beans, a couple of zucchini, and a handful of tomatoes from my backyard garden, my thoughts go back to earlier life on a Missouri farm. There we planted and harvested row after row of every vegetable imaginable, and gathered bushels of peaches, apples, and pears from the orchard on the hill.

By the time I was a teenager, I was the chief cook and canner, even Dad's farm "boy" in the fields, during the years of World War II. My four brothers were in the armed forces and my two sisters were married. I was the "baby" of seven children.

I worked in the kitchen until Dad would drive by the watering tank, stopping only long enough to let Prince and Lucy — our work horses — get a drink, and then he would call for me to join him at the hayloft. My arms weren't strong enough to pitch the hay from the wagon up into the barn window, so Dad pitched it up and I had the "easy" job of pushing it by pitchfork back to fill in all the corners of the loft.

With Missouri's 100-degree heat, chaff and dust filling the air, and no breeze coming through the window, those were long seasons of hay stacking!

One of the highlights of the summer of 1942 was the County Fair. I usually had to stay home and work, but for some reason this year I was invited to go along with some neighbors. Each of the other girls were taking some project which they'd made (canning, sewing, baking, etc.) to enter.

I had nothing available but Dad said, "Take a jar of peaches, you canned them." This I did. I dropped off my jar of peaches at the proper place, then hurried off with my friends to hear the singing and instrumental music competition. We ate our sack lunch at the proper time and the day passed much too quickly.

At four o'clock it was announced that we could pick up our entries as the judging was completed. Since we were farm folks, we had to be heading home to do the milking and other chores. So we left immediately to gather up whatever we'd taken there that morning.

When I arrived at the table of canned goods, I was

pleasantly surprised to see a blue ribbon taped to my jar of peaches.

Equally surprising was the realization that mine was the only half-gallon jar there!

Horse Trader's Daughter
by Cora Esch

western Iowa and eastern Nebraska, 1921-35

Until I was fourteen, I spent every summer traveling the eastern section of Nebraska and the western section of Iowa in a covered wagon. My father was a horse trader. After school was out in the spring, we would leave our Walthill, Nebraska, winter headquarters and go "on the road."

I can recall it all and make it as real as if I was in the covered wagon bumping along the unimproved roads of yesteryear. I can see the country school yard where we occasionally camped — and feel the delight of swinging high in the air on the old swing set, the joy of playing on the teeter-totter and slide that served as playground equipment for the children who attended the school. I can savor the cool, fresh water from the old hand pump and remember how good it tasted, after weeks of drinking water stored in ten-gallon cream cans.

Life of a road trader couldn't have been pleasant for my mother. Our living quarters was a structure about seven feet wide and ten feet in length. In this space was a small gas stove, cupboards for dishes, etc. The bed was built in the back of the wagon, with a trundle bed underneath.

Storage was over the bed.

In my memory's eye, I can see my mother as she cooked over an open fire when it was too hot to use the gas stove in the wagon. I remember her, quite often with a baby in her arms, as she drove the team of horses that pulled the covered wagon while my father and brother drove another wagon. I can still feel her work-worn hands as they stroked my hair, comforting me in a time of distress.

I can see Papa as he sat on a fallen log or a camp stool, whittling and whistling, as he waited for a local farmer who wanted to buy, sell, or trade horses to come into camp. I recall the friendly arguing, and sometimes the not-so-friendly bickering, the final settlement of the deal. I can feel the sense of complete happiness of my father at this time of his life.

I can recall the not-so-happy days that followed when the tractor replaced the horse for field work, and the need for work horses ceased to exist. I can still feel the frustration and anguish my father suffered when good work horses were sold for slaughter to be used in dog food, or for shipment overseas.

I can see my sister as she played with corn-silk dolls taken from the corn fields that grew along the shady land where we camped. I can hear the laughter of two small girls as we chased multicolored butterflies and tiny fireflies that seemed to hover just beyond our reach. I see the two of us as we sat in the shade of the giant oak trees that grew in abundance along the roadways, cutting paper dolls from a Sears-Roebuck catalog. I can see it all as if it was yesterday instead of sixty years ago.

I close my eyes and my brother, in his suspendered overalls, his straw hat pushed back on his head, is again herding horses along the grassy roadside of our camp site. I remember his kindness, his gentle teasing, and I remember well how he would tie a rope to a bucket handle, drop the bucket into one of the many creeks that flow in western Iowa, to fill the water barrels for the horses to drink.

I still shiver with anticipation as I remember the thrill of having the rope tied about my waist, to slowly descend into the creek. A sense of excitement runs through me yet, as I feel the clear cool water flow over my hot sweaty body.

Tears fill my eyes as I realize most of those I remember are gone.

I can almost hear the rain that fell against the canvas top of the wagon, making music only I could appreciate; I also remember the more violent storms when the men would hurriedly anchor the wagon with ropes fastened to hooks on the four corners of the wagon. They would secure them with iron stakes pounded into the ground, to keep the wagon from blowing over. I can hear the howling wind and feel the wagon swaying with its blast.

One of the more pleasant parts of our travels was seeing our old friends, people we visited each year. We always tried to be with the Parks family who lived just outside of Whiting, Iowa, over the Fourth of July. This was a break from the monotony of road living. To sleep in a soft bed while my friend slept in the camping buggy; to eat a meal, once again, in a house, or to have our friends share a meal with us in the camp area, helped the summer to go by quickly. By the end of August we were back in Walthill, in time for the Thurston county fair and to start the fall term of school.

I recall the love and appreciation I felt for these kind and generous people. I have felt, too, the lack of understanding by some. We were occasionally called gypsy; some farmers refused us permission to camp on their land. As my father said, "I don't blame them. They've probably been cheated by some trader going through the country. We'll move on to the next place where we're welcome."

While our standards have changed and there is no way to compare, I often wonder if I would be as charitable to a group of weary travelers as most people were to us.

I sincerely hope that should a group present themselves at my door, I will remember the kindness that was shown to us those many years ago and reciprocate with the same courtesy we received.

An August Dragon
by Sally Schnese

near Wild Rose, Wisconsin, early 1960s

Standing forlorn and forgotten on my father's farm is an old, gray, weather-beaten shed. On the outside it looks quite ordinary, not even worth a second glance. It's what's inside that makes it special.

Sure, there are people who've been in and out of there and will tell you that all they've seen is a rusty old threshing machine sitting quietly in the corner. But if you're curious enough to open the creaky doors and peer not only into the musty darkness of an old building but into a child's imagination as well, you may very well see it, too. I'm talking about a large, almost extinct breed of dragon!

While I was growing up, the highlight of my summer fell towards the end of my vacation, when the hot, still days of August rolled around. It was during that time that the warm evening breezes would begin to blow the fragrance of ripened grain through the holes and cracks of my father's old shed. I happened to know that such a smell was irresistible to grain-eating dragons.

Sure enough, pretty soon the old building would begin to bump and whine, as the beast inside slowly began to stir after a long year's rest. My excitement would grow, knowing that any day now, the dragon would peer out at me from underneath the slats of his shadowy cave.

After my father had announced his intentions of hauling the old fellow out, I'd get a seat safely out of the way to watch the battle between man and dragon. It would take at least two other men besides my father, and one very large, old tractor to coax him from his comfortable den. Most years he would come out quietly.

There were times, though, when he would become quite cantankerous and try to drag a corner of the old shed with him. Everything would come to a halt then, while the men carefully dragged him back inside and tried to make him straighten out and behave. I honestly think he looked a little pleased with himself whenever he could stir up some kind of mischief. But pleased or not, when he was finally out in the open and standing there under the eerie dusk of a summer's evening, he was a fearful sight to see!

Threshing was a busy time. One by one, many brightly colored pickup trucks would line our driveway as neighbors arrived to lend a hand. During those growing-up years, it was my job to run errands for my mother, as she hustled about preparing a huge dinner for the hungry threshing crew.

Between trips to the cellar for freshly canned vegetables and dill pickles, I'd keep one eye on my foe — the dragon — and one eye on the road. It was very important for me to be present when the dragon would eagerly munch down his first meal of the threshing season.

My patience was soon rewarded as a tall wagonload of golden bundles turned into the yard. I'd shiver with anticipation as my dad would fire up the big tractor, and the belts that held the old dragon prisoner would begin to move. At first, his huge hooked teeth would slowly grab at the bundles of grain the men threw to him, as if he wasn't really very interested.

Then as his rusty metal joints loosened up a bit, and he gradually worked off a year's worth of kinks, the teeth would move faster and faster, until the men could hardly pitch the stuff to him quickly enough.

The faster the powerful teeth would go, the more noise the dragon would make. Finally, even the loud shouts from among the men would be drowned out by the terrible dim of the dragon!

After I'd seen him gobble up quite a few bundles of grain, I'd scramble around to the back where the straw, now separated from the oats, would spew out into a nice fluffy stack. One man would have to be stationed there to direct the steady flow of straw and chaff. In my mind's eye, that man was actually a knight in shining armour, and the dust from the straw that completely enveloped us was the smoke from the fire-breathing dragon.

When at last the big wagonload of grain shocks was just about all fed to the beast, I'd hurry around to his side and hold my hands under the stream of oats that the old dragon would angrily spit out at us. They smelled like earth, and sunshine, and all the good things that I remembered most about living in the country. I'd always tuck a few safely away in my pockets, as if by doing so I could keep the magic of summer, and the dragon, alive for a little while longer.

The scene would be repeated many times during the next couple of days, until finally the last bundle was chewed up and swallowed. The fields, that had been checkered with shocks of oats only days before, now stood clean and empty.

The pies and cakes and other goodies my mother had worked so hard to prepare had all been eaten. And the crew of hard-working, good-natured men had packed up and moved on to the next farm to help someone else. It was a let-down to think that the magic was over for another year.

Yet, looking around at the towering mound of shimmering, golden straw in the barnyard, and the overflowing bins of earthy-smelling oats in the granary, it was easy to see that the magic of the August dragon would last all year long. My father could be content in the knowledge that all the farm animals would be well fed and snug during the long winter months ahead. It was with satisfaction that my foe the dragon returned to his dusty hiding place to rest up until next summer.

It's been years now since the old fellow has been called upon to do his job. Most farmers have replaced threshing machines with combines and other more modern kinds of farm equipment. Sadly enough, even dragons must get old and outlive their usefulness.

But the sights and sounds of that time are with me yet, and just as a familiar fairytale brings back pleasant childhood memories, so will I fondly recall the days of the August dragon.

My First Year of Teaching

Leona A. Buhlmann

Wheeler County, near Bartlett, Nebraska, 1936

"Oh, yes, Leona. I have the contract ready for you to sign as John and Dora signed it the other day." The director of the school board handed me a legal-looking form. I read through it, noting the penciled-in blanks which stated that I, Leona Melland, would teach for forty dollars a month for nine months, for a total sum of three hundred and sixty dollars.

After I had signed it, she handed me a black shoe-string on which were tied two keys — one for the school house and the other for a padlock on the coal-and-cob shed.

And so it was that I, at age seventeen and just having graduated from high school with a certificate in Normal Training, was given the responsibility of teaching in a one-room rural school.

The little white schoolhouse looked so lonely as it sat back from the trail road on the prairie grass. Behind it aways was a small long white shed which I knew would be the coal shed. Beyond that and spaced at opposite ends of the school yard were the two little "outhouses" or toilets. The doors of each were lettered with either a "B" or a "G"

— so no mistake should be made there!

The schoolhouse was "cracker box" in shape with an attached entry that had no windows. The entry wasn't locked, so I pushed open the door and stepped in. One wall had board shelves for the lunch buckets, and the other wall had nails for the coats and caps.

I unlocked the schoolhouse door and stood surveying the small room. Directly in front of me stood a "Round Oak" heating stove on a tin mat. It looked ornate with its fancy chrome trimmings. Beside it stood the coal bucket and the cob pail — my janitorial equipment.

My eyes were drawn to the front of the room, to the freshly painted blackboard which extended the breadth of the room. The chalk tray below it held long white sticks of chalk and two gray felt erasers. Above the blackboard were tacked long black cards with white letters showing the Palmer Method way of writing — a big capital "A" and the smaller "a" beside it. The entire alphabet was there to be copied neatly by the students.

Above the cards was a large picture of George Washington and, beside it, a small flag was neatly stapled to the wall displaying the blue field of forty-eight stars.

The teacher's desk seemed huge in that small room. On its top was a row of textbooks that were held firmly in place by metal bookends. On the edge of the desk was fastened a small pencil sharpener, with its glass case to catch the pencil shavings as the little crank made the roller grinders sharpen the pencil. Beside it was the small hand bell with a brass bottom and topped with a wooden handle.

A "teacher's chair" was tucked neatly under the desk. Drawers lined both sides of the desk for the supplies of penmanship paper, pencils, pen-holders with sharp metal tips, colors, and erasers. The long top drawer held the grade book, the lessons plan book, and the register of names in the district.

There were two rows of desks facing the teacher's desk. The smaller desks were nearest the front while the larger ones behind them were for the older grades. Since the desks were of one-piece construction, a seat was attached to the desk behind it. This sometimes left the smaller pupil sitting on a high seat with little legs dangling. That problem was solved by nailing an eight-inch-wide board between two 2-by-4s for a footrest.

The only other furniture was a wooden bench for recitations and a four-shelved bookcase that held surplus textbooks and a few library books.

I noticed the absence of a wall clock — I knew I would have to have a dependable watch.

The lighting wasn't the best. There were two windows on the west end and directly opposite on the east wall were two more windows. Green roller shades could be pulled down to shut out the glare on bright sunny days, but on dark cloudy days, they were rolled up to let in as much light as possible.

There was no well for water at the school, and the nearest available supply was a half-mile away. This meant that everyone would have to carry their drinking water to school every morning. The shiny tin syrup-pails with wire handles for carrying and a tight lid were used by everyone. The water might get warm during the day but it was wet!

If any water was left at the end of the school day, it was dumped into a three-gallon pail to be used in washing hands before lunch. Individually marked towels would be brought to school on Monday mornings and taken home to be washed on Fridays.

In order to teach that health lesson, I brought a tin wash-basin and a wooden orange crate for a stand. The soap was in an open dish to be used by everyone. (One weekend I discovered that most of the soap had been eaten by the mice. So it, too, had to be covered.)

What a challenge this school with all its shortcomings presented!

The School Day

"Discipline! That is the key word to your success in teaching."

That was the advice given to thirty-seven teachers as we met at the county courthouse in Bartlett in August for our supplies for the coming school term. "Establish your rules and stick with them."

The County Superintendent visited the rural schools unannounced several times during the school year. He checked our Course of Study, reviewed the written plans for each day in our plan book, and generally counseled if help was needed.

I made my rules! No whispering during school hours unless given permission. There was never to be two people out of their seats at one time. Hand signals were used: one finger to leave the room, two fingers to sharpen a pencil, and so on.

I answered questions between classes. (The lower grades could go to an older student for help with a reading word.)

The older students who finished their assignments early were allowed to help the little ones with flash-cards. How they both enjoyed that!

Grades were combined in teaching in the rural schools. On odd-numbered years, we taught the Nebraska Course of Study for the first, third, fifth, and seventh grades. On even-numbered years, the material for the even grades was taught. This helped give more time for classes.

Classes were hurried to a certain extent. Drilling with flash-cards on the arithmetic tables to see who could answer first was a speed game they enjoyed. A brief review over yesterday's work, and of course, the day's lesson, and then the assignment for the next day made the fifteen minutes fly. If individual help was needed, teacher was always available after school.

I enjoyed teaching penmanship. The red Palmer Method book started with "push-pulls" and "ovals" to loosen the arm muscle. Wood pencils were used in the lower grades, but wood pen-holders with removable metal tips that had to be dipped in ink wells were required for the older students. They took pride in their letter formation and in having a neat paper displayed on the school wall.

The classes in spelling followed so the "perfect letters" could be used. As I corrected their spelling words, I would comment on their writing.

After the last recess on Friday we had "art work." Decorations for the windows and school room were made by tracing patterns on construction paper or by coloring on white drawing paper.

Art work completed, the desks were cleaned and inspected. No messy desks allowed! This was the time for "spell downs" and "cipher downs" to see who was the champion for the week, so enthusiasm ran high.

The three Rs — reading, 'riting, and 'rithmetic — had to be mastered well. It was essential to getting out in the world.

In those days we weren't as impressed with "free-hand drawing" or "free expression." Pupils said, "Yes, Ma'am," and didn't question your authority.

The Economy in the 1930s

In the mid 1930s, our nation was suffering with the Great Depression, but this area also suffered with a drought.

The sandhills have an elusive beauty. The gently rolling hills are lush with grass in the springtime while the meadowlark's song fills the air. The prairies are dotted with colorful wildflowers. This seemed like such a promising land. The homesteaders staked out their claims and built homes. Too late they realized that the light soil should never have been plowed. The prairie winds whipped the grains of sand, and tender plants were cut off at the ground level.

One by one, the homesteaders abandoned their barren farms. The fields became areas of shifting sand, while the untouched prairie stretched for miles of fairly good grazing land.

The district where I was to teach had been hit especially hard. There were only five families left and they were struggling to make a living.

The necessities of food and clothing and a roof over their heads were the main concerns for themselves as well as their neighbors. They worked together, encouraging each other and helping with large tasks. Sharing a freshly butchered hog was common.

The main entertainment was visiting in the evenings.

Electricity was unheard of, so kerosene lamps lit their homes with a rosy glow. Radios were scarce and were powered by a six-volt battery from a car. This meant you chose your programs carefully as the battery ran out of power quickly. Newspapers weren't affordable, so neighbors gathering together shared state and national news as well as local news.

The pupils all walked to school. The farthest lived two miles from school and they were never late!

Their lunches were carried in the little tin Karo Syrup pails, too. The lids on these had nail holes for ventilation, though. In bitterly cold weather, those lunches arrived at the schoolhouse in frozen condition. This gave me the idea of putting a pan of water on top of the heating stove and setting little jars to heat in it. They brought pint jars with soup or cocoa and had a hot meal. The hot water was then used to wash at lunch time. When there was snow on the ground, I used it as water was scarce!

The teacher's economy? Well, I had been warned, "Don't expect to save any money until after Christmas," and I found that to be true. There were always needed supplies that you hated to ask the director to buy, so you bought them yourself.

I realized that most of my upper-grade pupils would not be financially able to go to high school. They would "hire out" as hired girls or hired men in the neighborhood, so I tried to instill in them some "self worth." I wanted to impress on them the character traits of honesty, integrity, and respect.

Every Monday morning I wrote either a proverb or wise saying on the blackboard which we read together, after pledging the flag and singing "America." One wise saying was: "There is no gray line for honesty. It is either black or it is white. It is either wrong or it is right." I hoped they would remember these proverbs and sayings when difficult times came.

I taught the girls to crochet when there was time and they were finished with studies. A new hobby for them!

The Day I Lost It

One of my regrettable days the first year I taught school was the day I lost my temper and spanked!

In those days, though, the parents sent their children off to school with the warning, "If you get a spanking at school, you'll get a harder one when you get home." It was "Be good or else."

My trouble started when I refused my little first grader's decision to take home his reading book.

In the mid-1930s, we taught reading by the "sight method." Flash cards with words were learned — the first word being "Dick." The next word, "see," and another card had "run" on it. "Jane," "Spot," and "come" were also learned.

By placing the cards together on the chalk tray, we

had a story: "See Dick run, see Jane run, see Spot run." Finally, they were given the book "Dick and Jane" with its colorful pictures and they were reading!

Dickie, my little first grader, was quick at learning and asked if he might take his book home to "show Mama how I can read."

The next day he read perfectly — even using a reading tone, but as I glanced at his page, I saw he was reading from the wrong page! He had memorized the story so he wasn't really reading.

"Dickie, you have shown your mama your book so don't take it home anymore," I requested.

That afternoon when I dismissed the pupils I noticed an odd bulge under Dickie's shirt.

"Dickie," I said as I reached under his shirt and pulled out the book, "You weren't to take that home. Go put it back in your desk."

His temper flared. "I am too going to take it home, G__ D__ You!" His words shocked the rest of the pupils and me, too.

"Dickie, those are naughty words and you will have to sit in your seat now for five minutes before you go home."

"I will not! I'm going home." I caught him by his arm and, with him resisting all the way, I brought him back to his desk. But would he sit? No! He slid out the other side and started for the door again. Putting him back in his seat started more screaming and cursing.

He fell to the floor with a perfect temper tantrum, and I, wonderfully calm, lifted him and placed him back in his seat. Again he slid out and this time, he took out his revenge on the artwork that had been tacked on the wall. It flew in all directions as he raged along the wall.

I was still calm as I knelt to pick up some "treasured art" when I heard one of the pupils call, "Miss Leona, look out!" Out of the corner of my eye I saw a tear-streaked, red-faced Dickie with his wooden footstool held high above his head and determination in his eyes as he aimed the blow at my head. I lost my calm! I didn't even stand! I reached over and with one arm I flipped him over my knee and paddled that little seat with my bare hand.

It broke that rebellious spirit because when I placed him in his seat that time, he put his head down on his desk and cried brokenheartedly.

"All right, Dickie," I said, "you have sat your five minutes so you may go home now. Just remember never to use those naughty words again."

He took his dinner pail and walked slowly and sadly out the door.

I turned to clean the school room, picking up the scattered wall-hangings and smoothing the torn parts. I was sick with remorse. How could I have lost my cool so completely? How would I be able to face the pupils in the morning? I wondered what they were telling their parents. They had all witnessed the spanking but had left when I requested that they go home.

I heard the noise of a car pulling onto the school yard and, glancing out, I recognized Dickie's folks' car. I'll never forget that moment! I went to the schoolroom door just as Dickie and his father reached it.

Dickie's dad, his big western hat pushed back from his forehead, had a quizzical grin as he looked at me.

"Miss Leona, I have a little boy here who says he was naughty and he wants to tell you he's sorry and give you a kiss and ask if you'll forgive him." The dad's hand was on little Dickie's shoulder as if to give him courage. Dickie looked so tearfully at me that I stooped and held out my arms to him and received the warmest hug and kiss a little boy could give.

Yes, I apologized too!

Games in the Mid-'30s

Rural school pupils were as eager for recess as their city cousins. The teacher, too, appreciated the opportunity to teach character traits — honesty, fairness, and consideration for others. This was so true because in rural schools, all ages played together.

"Pom-pom pull-away" was a favorite active game in which everyone joined. There were two bases and one "It," until he caught some of the runners who then joined him in catching others.

Another favorite game was "Anti-i-over." The little

crackerbox schoolhouse was ideal for the game. Sides were chosen and each side took one side of the schoolhouse. A rubber ball was tossed over the schoolhouse while everyone hollered "Anti-i-over." The ball should not be allowed to touch the ground! There was a mad scramble for that ball, and the one who caught it gathered his group together and chose one person to carry the ball.

Racing around the sides of the schoolhouse, the ball carrier attempted to touch as many from the other side as he could. A fast person could catch quite a few who then were on their side. Sometimes the ball wasn't caught, so it was tossed back over. No fair, though, if they didn't warn by calling, "Anti-i-over." (A consideration: let one of the little ones carry the ball.)

A not-so-active game was "May I." A leader would draw a straight line in the sand and have all the players toe the line. As each player's name was called, the leader would say, "Cecil, you may take two baby steps forward." Cecil would ask, "May I?" and step forward. If he forgot, the leader would send him back to the line. For the next little one, the leader might say, "Dickie, you may take three giant steps forward." Sometimes it was hard to accept the leader's decisions but it taught tolerance.

"New Orleans" was a creative game. Sides were chosen and, after consulting together as a "side," they would choose some activity to demonstrate — such as "making a cake." Advancing to the other side, the group would call,

"Here we come," and the other side would ask, "Where are you from?" The response of "New Orleans" was questioned by "What's your trade?" "Butter and eggs" was the reply. Then, "Get to work and show us some if you're not afraid." Each player would act out his idea of preparing a cake. The group guessing would have to use the exact wording of "making a cake," and when it was guessed, the actors would run back to their base while the other side tagged as many as possible. They then joined that group and planned a new activity.

A quiet game to stimulate memory retention was one I used as they ate their lunches. (One rule was that they sat in their seats for fifteen minutes whether they were eating or not.) It was called the alphabet game and started by one person who said, "I went to the store and bought some apples." The next in line would add, "I went to the store and I bought some apples and beans." The third person repeated the list and added something starting with "c." Our aim was to get through the entire alphabet without forgetting an item.

Another game was "My grandmother can't drink tea but she can drink apple juice." (Because "tea" ends with an "a," the next drink had to begin with "a." Since juice ends with an "e," the next drink had to begin with an "e," such as eggnog.) This brought out some imaginative and unpalatable drinks!

The homonym game was one for rainy or stormy days.

Everyone suggested homonyms which I wrote on the blackboard (such as son — sun, blue — blew, and so on). Each would choose one and make up a sentence such as "I bought a ____ kite but it ____ away." The challenge was to guess the homonym. Or course, after they knew their homonyms, the words were erased for it wasn't so easy. They composed sentences with many homonyms, "My ____ wanted to be a ____ but he couldn't stand the ____ so he had to go out to work at ____."

Of course baseball in the spring was great. Everyone had a turn at pitching the rubber ball — even the first graders! A flat board of a handy size was the bat. There were no sides—it was just an achievement to hit the ball or be able to throw it to another player. Rules weren't mentioned — just cooperate and encourage each player.

"Hide and Go Seek" wasn't too much of a challenge. The only places to hide were behind the outhouses, coal shed, and the schoolhouse.

Winter games required a lot of bundling up, but that fresh cold air that brought rosy cheeks and new incentives to study was worth the extra chores. The game "Fox and Geese" waited until a deep snow covered the playground. Traveling behind a leader, a big circle was stomped out and then divided diagonally with a smaller circle reserved for the geese home base. The "geese" would venture out on the paths and taunt the fox who would race after them. If he caught one, it became a fox, too, until all were caught.

Of course building huge snowmen families was fun. Throwing snowballs was inevitable — but there were rules! "No hard balls! Throw only at bodies or legs — not heads!"

Stocking caps, jackets, and mittens had to be hung around the heating stove to dry before they could be worn for the long, cold walk to their homes.

As you notice, we did not have play equipment at all. A ten-cent rubber ball was the only investment. The group games took ingenuity and they learned cooperation. We were democratic in choosing what to play — and perhaps, the next day their favorite games would be chosen.

Special Events

The two big social events that brought patrons, relatives, and acquaintances from near and far were the Christmas program and the school picnic.

Several months before Christmas I scanned little booklets of "School Plays and Recitations" to choose suitable performances for each child. It was important that each child have a "piece to speak" and to perform in a little play.

The schoolroom, too, was to take on a festive look. I bought red and green crepe paper and cut the material into two-inch-wide strips. By tacking one end of a strip to a corner and twisting the strips slightly, I stretched it to a diagonal corner and tacked. In the center where the strips crossed, we hung a tissue fold-out bell. Aluminum icicles were then hung on the strips.

Imagine my surprise when I entered the schoolhouse the next morning to find the paper strips hanging at waist-level! When the heating stove dried and warmed the room, the strips shrunk back and were above our heads again.

Christmas trees sold for fifty cents but the majority of the homes would not be able to buy one, so we made the "school tree" special. The pupils used red and green construction paper to make ring chains. Folding aluminum scraps into shapes and hanging them where the sun's rays made them sparkle was exciting. We also strung popcorn and draped that among the branches. A shiny foil star topped the little tree.

During our art periods on Friday we made gifts to give the parents. The boys and girls both learned to sew as they made hot pads for their mothers. I had taken some school photos earlier in the year and these were put on calendars for their dads.

The pupils had drawn names so that everyone would receive a gift. The price limit was twenty-five cents — a big sum if there were three or more children in a family.

We started practicing when everyone had memorized their parts. When practice began, the teacher became a director, producer, and stage manager. (Sad to say, but a lot of people judged the teacher by her Christmas program!)

Preparing the stage took some ingenuity, too. Heavy clothesline wire was stretched across the front of the room. White sheets were pinned over the wire. Side wires that were hung with more sheets formed "dressing rooms" for the actors to change costumes.

Producing a program was a time when discipline counted. No noise was allowed behind the curtains because there usually was someone in front of the curtain reciting their "piece" while the rest prepared the stage for the next production.

The program was usually planned for forty-five minutes to an hour with songs, plays, and recitations. After that there would be a jingling of bells, a loud knock at the door, and a "ho-ho" Santa appeared.

I had bought the Santa outfit and asked a neighbor to play Santa. Believe me, that was the hardest job of all! The children helped pass the gifts as Santa's mask kept slipping over his eyes so he was "snow-blind."

That year I bought a bushel of apples for Santa and his helpers to pass to the crowd. A lunch of sandwiches and cookies was brought by the families and enjoyed with lots of visiting.

The school picnic, too, brought lots of good food and sharing of recipes because this was a community affair.

After the bountiful meal where everyone filled his plate with a "little sampling" of everything until their plates were heaping, the children were ready for games.

One game that brought lots of laughter and joshing was the sack race. I prepared large paper sacks, each with an article of old clothes — a corset in one, long underwear in another, and so on. Anything ridiculous went into those sacks.

The two teams lined up and, one at a time, would race to the sacks, choose one, and put that piece of clothing on regardless of whether it fit or not. (Imagine a booted man trying to get into a ladies slip!) Amid cat-calls and laughter, he would race back to the line, and another contestant would "dress" for the occasion.

One that the children enjoyed was the gunny sack race with each contestant jumping as fast as he could in the big sack to the goal line. There were lots of tumbles!

The race that the women enjoyed seeing was one where the men were handed a pillow case and a pillow and were told to put it on, take it off, and hand it to the next in line. Some of the men used their teeth to hold the case and "knocked" the pillow in with their fists!

The men got even, though, when the women were to pound three nails into a 2x4-inch board. In the excitement and cheering, some of them couldn't hit the nail!

The Brush Arbor Meetin'
by Billie M. Mauler

Ozark County, near Gainesville, Missouri, 1943

"Are you goin' to the meetin' tonight?" was the question asked a dozen times that day from one child to another in the little one-room school we all attended.

"My dad cut the poles for the arbor," one boy exclaimed proudly.

"Well, my dad and Uncle Jim made all the seats," piped up another.

"I helped my dad cut the brush for the roof," one of the bigger boys chimed in.

The community was astir. A lady preacher named Mae Starling had come into our midst and wanted to hold a revival meetin'.

The hard-shelled Baptists and the Cambellites (that's what my grandmother called them) were up in arms. A woman preacher! No siree, no woman preacher in our church!

Their church was actually our schoolhouse. Preachers were scarce. A community could not support a regular pastor. So the preacher would serve several communities. Working through the week like the rest of the folks on their own small farms, they would hold services on Sunday at the schools on a rotating basis, which meant we had church about once a month.

We never knew how the lady preacher came to be in our parts. Some allowed the Lord must have sent her, so several men and boys, who must not have been of either persuasion, Baptists or Cambellites, set to work and built a brush arbor.

It was a simple structure. Four large posts were set at each corner braced with smaller posts. Boards were nailed to the tops of the posts to make a frame for the roof. Small bushes, or brush as they were called, were used to fill in empty spaces. A large tree would be cut down and sawed into pieces. These chunks would be stood on end and used to support long smooth boards. These were the pews. A shorter one would be placed near the front of the structure. This was "the mourner's bench," or altar.

We hurried through chores and supper and joined our neighbors heading for the meetin'. There were very few cars in South Central Missouri in the early 1940s. Most folks were walking the dirt roads. Some with very small children took their horses and wagons, and a few were on horseback. My sister and I felt very dressed up in our pretty print flour-sack dresses Mother had made for us, as we hurried to keep up with the others.

It was almost dark when we arrived. There was no electricity but each family had brought their "coal oil" (kerosene) lantern. These were hung on nails on the posts and filled the arbor with light. They also attracted a large assortment of flying insects but everyone was so taken with the lady preacher they scarcely noticed anything else.

Mae Starling was a very attractive woman in her middle thirties, with long dark hair arranged in a becoming bun at the nape of her neck. She was definitely a "city woman," everyone decided, eyeing her lovely "store bought" dresses and stylish shoes.

She was wearing an accordion which she began to play very skillfully and her singing was like that of an angel. Then she spoke in a soft warm voice telling of a God that loved and wanted to give his spirit unto us. Not the hellfire and brimstone sermons we were used to hearing.

The revival lasted for two weeks. The brush arbor was filled to capacity every night. Many came and stayed in the shadows just to observe. The hills resounded with music and singing and the shouts of newborn believers as they prayed around the altar. In the midst of them, down in the dirt and sawdust oblivious of her beautiful clothes, was the lovely evangelist.

There was a baptizing in the creek on Sunday and then she was gone. The Baptists and Cambellites snorted "good riddance," some basked in the afterglow, and others were glad to get back to normal.

One of the new converts back in school, tormented by the other boys about getting religion, came forth with a volley of every bad word he ever heard, to prove he didn't really have religion after all.

Other brush arbor meetings were held in years following — but none as memorable as the one held by the beautiful lady preacher.

The Dinner Bucket

by Kathryn E. McGaughey

Prairie Hill school, near Broken Bow, Nebraska, 1925-1933

While working in the modern kitchen of the school cafeteria and sloshing all the leftovers down the disposal, I thought how fortunate these children of this modern age are today. They'll never know the surprises that a cold "dinner bucket" could contain.

Early in this century (1920s and 1930s) before a hot-lunch program was even thought of or conceived, it was necessary to carry lunch to school. I doubt if lunch boxes were even available and if they were, they were an item that we could do without. Money was scarce on the farm in middle Nebraska. Most students walked one to three miles to school and, of course, it was impossible to go home for lunch, so we all carried a five or ten-pound lard bucket filled with surprising contents.

One student had a grandfather who chewed "Tiger" Tobacco. It came in a five-by-ten-inch square tin with handles on each side that folded down and made a good lunch bucket. We were all envious of that bucket because it had a large colorful picture of a tiger on it, where ours just had some plain red lettering on one side.

No thought was given to a balanced diet or caloric

intake (the morning walk took care of that), but rather what was convenient on the pantry shelf at home.

Sunday was always a day of feasting. Sometimes the preacher came for dinner, so Monday's lunch bucket was filled to the brim with goodies. There might be fried chicken or wild rabbit, a slab of pie, or a doughnut (homemade, naturally), or gingerbread, or a cupcake, and usually one of Mama's juicy, dripping, dill pickles from the crockery jar in the cellar.

The everyday normal bill of fare was jelly sandwiches. To this day I cannot really relish grape jelly because of all the wild grapes picked in the canyons and preserved during the early years of my life. There was grape jelly, grape pie, grape conserve, and when we were sick with a fever — we got grape juice.

Peanut butter was a scarce commodity. With cattle selling for nineteen dollars a head and hogs bringing two dollars and fifty cents for a hundred pounds, we didn't buy unnecessary items. Peanut butter was considered such an item. I am sure there are mothers today that would argue that point.

In the spring of the year when the hens were laying nearly every day, we had hard-boiled eggs in our lunch, shells included. A sprinkling of salt was carefully wrapped in a bit of brown waxed paper that had come from the store and was smoothed and folded to be used day after day, because there were no rolls of clear plastic or foil or sandwich bags to make our lunches more palatable.

Did you ever eat a cornbread sandwich? It is very filling with salt pork. A cold baking-powder biscuit is equally as tasty, but a professional dietician would probably regard it with horror as a meal for growing children.

One teacher devised a plan whereby we could bring from home a jar of soup or some other nourishing goody, place it in a pan of water on the pot-bellied stove during the first recess, and by noon, we would have a hot meal. However, this came to a sudden halt when a jar blew up midway between recess and noon, and bits of carrot, onion, and "what have you" were plastered from the ceiling to the blackboard.

One winter, my grandparents from Washington sent a box of enormous red apples. They lasted for a glorious month and were the envy of every other dinner-bucket carrier in the school. I relished each tasty mouthful, eating long and loud for everyone's benefit. I'm sure everyone, including the teacher, was especially glad when the supply was depleted.

Trading lunches was a noon pastime.

"Trade ya' my boiled egg for your gingerbread."

"Trade ya' my doughnut for your sandwich."

But one young student was always avoided in the swapping episode. It was discovered by a regrettable mistake that his sandwiches were nothing but coarse, home-made bread spread lavishly with not-too-freshly rendered lard! He was a tall, lanky kid with a ravenous appetite, and he devoured them as though they were oysters on the half shell. I wonder what became of him? Last I heard of him he was running for the legislature, and I doubt if that bulge in his pocket was a lard sandwich.

One year when there was no water at school, we had to carry another lard bucket filled with water. The weather was extremely frigid and as I carried both buckets and a book tucked under my arm I became very cold. I had nearly a mile to walk, and when I got to the schoolhouse the bucket of water was frozen solid and my hands remained in the shape where I had held the wire handles, for an hour or more. No doubt, I suffered frostbite.

The "buckets" were always arranged on a wooden bench under the coat rack. Some had red lettering, some were bent and bashed beyond recognition, but none were alike. Each was as individual as its owner. Quite a contrast to the well-balanced meals that are scooped from warm steam-tables, served on warm sterile plates amid perfect conditions. But very few leftovers went home in the "dinner bucket," and if they did they were consumed on the way home. No corner drugstore for after-school snacks.

So, I'll just slosh the leftovers down the disposal and wish that just one day, these youngsters could know the surprise that a ten-pound lard "dinner bucket" might contain.

Patrick

by William A. McGaughey

Victoria Township, near Anselmo, Nebraska, 1931

Late one evening in October of 1931, Mother and my sister were doing the supper dishes. Dad was reading the *Daily Omaha World Herald.* My brother and I were doing our homework. We were both students in high school. My brother was working on his math and I was reading a book that was compulsory for English. Our dog was lying under the table curled up by my feet.

Suddenly, he sat up and uttered a deep growl from his throat. Pup was half coyote and half collie. Most dogs have extremely good hearing, but Pup had even more sensitive hearing. He went to the kitchen door and stood there listening. It was then I heard the rattle of stay chains on a harness and the squeak of dry wagon hubs.

Soon I heard footsteps and I knew someone was approaching the porch. It was a dark night and all I could see was a shadow of someone coming up the porch steps, nearing the kitchen door. I opened the inside door and a man's voice spoke, asking for the man of the house. I called to Dad who came up beside me. As Dad opened the screen door, Pup growled, and it was necessary for me to grab him by the scruff of the neck to keep him from attacking the person on the porch.

The man said, "I have traveled thirty miles or more today looking for work. My horses and I are tired and I would be glad to work for room and board for myself and my horses until corn-picking time.

Dad said, "Son, go with this man and help him put his horses in the barn."

We approached the team and the man spoke gently to them. We unhitched them, took them to the water tank where the thirsty pair drank the cool water with gusto. We led them into the barn and as we pulled the harness and collars off the tired team, I noticed raw sores on their shoulders and necks. I gave him the Rawleigh's all-purpose salve and he spread a generous portion on the sores of each horse. I got a can of oats and put one in each feed box for the horses. I climbed up into the haymow and forked down several forks full of hay into the manger of each horse. The horses ate hungrily.

When we got back into the house, Mother had bacon and eggs frying and the aroma of coffee wafted toward us as we entered the kitchen door. I poured a pan of warm water from the reservoir into the wash basin on the wash stand, and our visitor gratefully washed his hands and face and combed his hair. My sister had set a plate, cup and saucer with silverware on the table, and I poured him a cup of the steaming hot coffee. I sat the pitcher of cream by his plate and he thanked me but he said he took his coffee without sugar or cream.

After eating, he said he would get his bedroll and sleep in the haymow. Mother assured him that we had a spare bedroom and it was a little cool to sleep in the barn. His soft voice and good manners soon won us over and we took him in as one of the family.

He borrowed some of my extra clothes so Mother could wash and patch his shirt and overalls. On the first Saturday that we went to town, Dad bought him a new chambray shirt and a pair of bib Oshkosh overalls and underwear and socks that he desperately needed.

Because it wasn't quite corn-picking time, Dad was glad to have an extra hand to help around the farm. While we were in school, he helped Dad muck out the horse and cow barns and haul the manure and spread it on the stubble field and sandy knolls. The corn cribs and granaries needed to be checked and repaired for the fall harvest, and wagons needed to be greased and gotten ready for the long days of picking corn. Each wagon had a bangboard on one side where the ears of corn were thrown and, as the name implies, bang on the board and fall into the wagon. Because Dad was left-handed, his bangboards had to be placed on the opposite side.

The fields were laid out, one third for the landlord and two thirds for us. The landlord's corn had to be shucked. But we left the shucks on our corn — this is called "snapping" — and fed it to the animals on the farm.

Patrick picked ours and Dad shucked the corn for the landlord.

After our corn crop was all harvested, Patrick went to help the neighbors but he returned each night to our house. He even helped my brother and me with our homework which raised our grades from a C to a B and B+. He seemed to be a well-educated person. He always was willing to help with the chores, slopping the hogs and milking the twenty cows which took a lot of heavy work from Dad and us boys. He stayed on with us until spring.

One Sunday we invited him to go with us to church and Sunday school and after that he attended regularly. Because of his friendly ways, he became acquainted with most of our neighbors in the community.

One Sunday our regular minister was late. He was an interim minister and had another country church where he preached before coming to ours. The audience was becoming restless waiting, and Patrick asked permission to speak with us.

Naturally, the audience gave their permission, and Patrick strode to the pulpit, opened his well-worn bible, and read the 23rd Psalm. He spoke in a quiet manner about love for your neighbor. And halfway through his sermon, our regular minister and his wife came in the door quietly. With a quick glance, he could see someone had taken his place so they sat down in the back row and listened intently. When Patrick finished, our minister was the first one to congratulate him and shake his hand.

Patrick stayed with us until spring, selling his team and wagon, and boarded the train. He never said where he was going or what he intended to do, but we wished him well.

Four years later, there was a picture and an article in the daily paper about Patrick, and it was then that we finally knew his full name. All we had ever known about him was his first name, but the picture was a true likeness and we recognized him immediately. He had attended a seminary and graduated as a minister.

Nine years later in another state, I met a man on a street in a city and as we met, we both turned and recognized each other at once. It was Patrick. We spent an hour on a park bench visiting and reminiscing about those hard times when he came to our house cold and hungry.

It was the last I knew anything of him until many years later after my marriage, when we had moved to a large city. There in the daily paper was Patrick's obituary. He had realized his dream and became the minister of a large church.

Memories of Sheepherding

by Herman Hammel

Dunn County, near Killdeer, North Dakota, 1933

It was a nice spring day in 1933. Brother Bobbie and I were going along with Pa to Killdeer, North Dakota, in the grain wagon to get new shoes. We had grown out of our old worn school shoes, being both rambunctious boys of eleven and thirteen years. Our job would be herding the sheep flock out on the range.

Pa was in good spirits too, as he was to pick up his seed wheat for spring planting. His government loan had been approved. The thoughts of a "bumper wheat crop" would set up Pa in good standing with his banker. Pa's faith and optimism was contagious.

Our ranch of about three thousand acres was on the edge of the Badlands and well suited for sheep and cattle. Pa was a good livestock man and knew farming too. With our flock of eight hundred ewes, the fenced sheep pasture of a half section was literally a "Big Sheep Corral."

Since Bobbie and I were the youngest of five brothers, the job of herding sheep was elected to us. The three older boys had more responsibility of the farming and haying work.

Outfitted with new shoes and overalls, Pa announced

that "You two boys will be the sheep herders for the summer." We felt proud and grown up and we also knew our responsibilities of herding, already having had some of that experience.

With our personal saddle horses, Bobbie on "Blue" and I on "Dan," we knew we'd have some good times too. With our good sheep dog "Pal," we were confident and equal to the challenge.

When our rural school was closed for the summer, Bobbie and I were anxious to get started. The adjoining school section that we leased from the state would be our main herding area for the summer. The sheep would have a bedground at the far end of the fenced pasture. Here, every morning at a gate, we'd let them out to scatter and graze during the day. The lambs would get fat for the fall market in South St. Paul.

Sheep are always hungry and will graze until satisfied. By then, they are thirsty and will head for the nearest water and shade. The Boggy Spring is centered in this area, and the sheep would lay up there to rest in the shade of the popple groves for a couple of hours, enabling Bobbie and me to head home for a quick meal on our saddle horses.

We would always return to the sheep immediately. Most of the afternoon we'd have time to play at a cut bank on a hillside, and from this vista we could also watch the sheep. Here, at this cut bank we had our "Stick Horse

Ranch," digging with sticks into the clay bank to make our "Ranch Headquarters." With our jack knives, we'd cut birch saplings to ride for stick horses and make an elaborate set of corrals with sticks. Our ingenuity and imagination were our only limitations. Many, many hours were spent here throughout the summer at play.

After some hot days in June, we were ready for shearing sheep. The grease in the wool was at its maximum. The sheep were not herded during the shearing weeks. We would run a bunch in for the afternoon shearing and turn out the ones kept overnight for the noon clip. The shearers would travel from farm to farm.

Part of my job was to cut strings that tied the wool. Another chore was being water boy for fifteen thirsty shearers. The job we loathed was sacking wool. The wool sacks were three feet wide and seven feet long. We had a four-legged derrick that the sack hung from, secured by a round metal hoop threaded through the top seam of the sack. The top of the sack was attached to the hoop much the same as a curtain is threaded on a curtain rod.

The sack hung down and one boy would tramp wool inside the sack while another dropped fleece into the sack. This was a hot and greasy job, especially when one brother dropped fleece on top of the other brother's head. Tempers flared. We would disappear from the sheep shed on any excuse.

Three miles from the home place we had the Jim Creek Camp. It was my grandfather's original homestead, purchased in 1896. Pa acquired it in 1923. This is where we put up most of our hay on the creek bottom. While the three older brothers and Pa would put up hay, we'd take the sheep down there and herd along Jim Creek and the Chimney Butte Creek area. That amounted to an additional three sections of pasture land. In the old log house, we'd "batch it" and go home only on weekends.

Some weeks, either Bobbie or I would have to help Pa and our older brothers with the haying. The job involved raking the prairie hay with the ten-foot dump rake. Haying was dusty and dirty. Evenings we'd all gather after bachelor supper and take a swim in Jim Creek. The swimming hole was close to our camp, where Chimney Butte Creek ran into Jim Creek at a ninety-degree angle. Flood waters had made a nice sandbar to undress on.

Saturday nights we'd quit early to take our swim and be up at the home place where Mother would have a bountiful supper waiting for us. What a treat the fresh garden produce was after batching it all week, mostly on boiled potatoes and cured meat.

We had a lot of fun at that swimming hole. Seeing Pa naked shocked me at first, but after all he was just like us five boys and joined in the fun of throwing mud and water. The camaraderie and horseplay endeared us to Pa and helped us all over some rough and hard times to come.

Some weeks Bobbie had to be "Man of the home place" and help Mother in the garden with our two younger sisters. Herding sheep alone, I began to examine nature and amuse myself in whatever I could think of. I hunted for arrowheads and luckily found a few good specimens of Knife River flint at some old Indian tepee rings.

I split some fractured sand rock and inside found some nice leaf fossils. High on a butte I found a petrified freshwater clam. I found some petrified fish bones in a fractured scoria rock. I was interested and read and learned about the geological world. This whole area had been dinosaur country fifty million years ago.

Being alone I felt in tune with nature. Sometimes I could feel a presence that I was being watched. I might turn around, and there only a few yards away amongst the sheep would be a mother antelope. She might be hesitant to leave, having a fawn hidden close by. Seeing the sheep dog, she becomes very agitated. She trots to a small rise and stamps her feet. Running in small circles, she whistles shrilly. The two white bars across her throat look like snowy white scarves. After regaining my composure from the excitement of her presence, I talk to her and tell her not to be afraid.

The sheep move on in their grazing, and from a distance, I see her go back and rouse her fawn. A most beautiful sight in their graceful swiftness of flight — the sight fills me with wonder and awe.

Another very memorable experience was while herding the flock in Coal Mine Draw. There is a high narrow ridge down the middle, forming a forked valley having a small cut bank high on the sunny side. Just below this cut bank, about six antelope had taken rest after their feeding time. The wind was right for me to circle a long way around without being seen or scented, and come up from the back side of the ridge overlooking the cut bank.

After careful maneuvering, I crept up to the cut bank very slowly and quietly looked down upon the family of antelope. The large old buck sensed the presence of something watching him. He turned his head and I was mesmerized by the details of his magnificent head. His large ebony eyes stared at me with intensity.

Frozen moments passed. I did not even blink my eyes for fear that he would alert and be gone. His large obsidian nostrils flared, and with a shrill whistle, his whole body sprang into action. Instantly he was bounding down the slope with his harem following. I was spellbound; what had just transpired seemed almost unreal. I sat down to control my excitement. Never shall I forget those moments of fascination, my heart was thumping like a trip hammer. That evening I was still euphoric in telling about my experience.

An area that intrigued both Bobbie and me was the Burning Coal Mine over on South Creek. Some years ago a lightning strike had ignited an outcropping seam of coal on this hillside. It had burned back under the overburden of sod and just kept on smoldering without flame, with just enough air to keep up combustion.

Pa had warned us not to go near there as sections of the hillside had caved in due to the burned-out coal underneath. There was also the danger of rattlesnakes. The warm earth attracted voles and mice, which the snakes lived on.

We however were curious and had to satisfy ourselves about exactly where the smoke came out of the cracks. On a cool morning, light smoke hung in the atmosphere and we could tell exactly where it came out of the ground. The main hole was about six inches in diameter and we warmed our hands over the hole. After satisfying our curiosity, it held no more allurement for us.

It was never any threat for a prairie fire. The sheep and other livestock seemed to avoid grazing the area. It had at that time burned underground about two acres.

We killed every rattlesnake that we found. They bite several sheep every summer and it's seldom that a sheep survives.

The voices of nature were everywhere in the Badlands over the sheep range. Stopping to listen, there were the songs of birds. The meadowlarks were plentiful. One long-winded bird sang for almost ten minutes. His pure and distinct melody rippled with notes as clear and beautiful as silver bells. That really helped my attitude and I would sing the best I knew how. One of my favorites was "When It's Springtime in the Rockies." It had just come out over the radio from which I had memorized the words.

Prairie chickens were plentiful on our ranch. Their main diet were the birch catkins and buffalo berries in the wintertime. A covey could usually be found in a berry patch. Hundreds would gather at their booming grounds in early spring to perform their courtship dances. The roosters inflated their air sacs up to the size of a lemon on the sides of their head. Then they would strut around with wings drooped and produce a booming sound that could be heard for a mile or more. I observed their antics up quite close in a secluded brush patch. I witnessed a grand display on this hillside of about two acres.

They are very pretty birds with striped bars of brown and black on a gray body. These earthy colors make them blend well with the prairie grass in which they nest.

In the wintertime we trapped some for eating. Their meat is delicate and fine of dark texture. It sure was good stew and made for a welcome variety in our meat diet.

The summer of 1933 was hot and dry. The days melted into each other with relentless wind to further dry out the parched grain fields. There was stunted corn and scant grain out on the flat farm lands. We fared better on the Jim Creek Bottoms, which seemed like an oasis.

I would herd the sheep until almost dark before corralling them. I could watch the sunsets on the horizon. Dust and smoke hanging in the atmosphere from distant Montana forest fires made the sky a deep crimson red. The sky was ever-changing with the lowering sun. Bands of gold and mauve streaked the horizon. As the sun dropped, the colors lessened in intensity and spread in pastel diffusion.

These sunsets were very enjoyable. My thoughts were that I was living in a wonderful world. Through my youthful eyes, the worldly affairs of men seemed almost unimportant.

There are many buttes on the Hammel and adjoining range, but Chimney Butte towers above the rest. It is the highest elevation for miles around. It was the mecca of my boyhood. I spent many, many hours on top watching over the sheep as they grazed the creek valley for up to a mile or more. It was also a favorite spot for visitors to come and enjoy the beautiful panorama including a good vista of Killdeer Mountains.

Watching the lazy billowing clouds drift by, I would be carried in my imagination to marvelous places that I had read about.

It was here that I found peace in the harmony of land and nature. This old butte seemed to be attuned to my life whatever was my mood. Looking back in retrospect, I realize that my sheep-herding experiences were in a large

114

part the make-up of my spiritual development.

For centuries the old butte has stood, unmoved by the wind, rain, snow, freezing cold, and heat. It may have secrets inside, maybe bones of prehistoric creatures. If only if it could talk, what tales of history it could reveal.

Steadfast, the old sentinel overlooks the present Hammel ranch now in the fourth generation of stewardship.

Blackboards, Syrup Pails, and Tassel Caps

by Marilyn Brinkman

Stearns County, near St. Martin, Minnesota, 1949-1955

My grade-school memories are like a beautiful far-reaching tree, planted while I was a child. I feel I was born at the end of the pioneering era when days were miles long; when nature showed us how to have fun; when family, home, and friends taught us values and goals; and our teachers enlarged those values and goals.

At the end of my 1955 school year, after my year as a seventh grader, my one-room schoolhouse closed. An era in history ended for me with the closing of Independent School District Number 81 in St. Martin, Minnesota.

Now and then I drift back in time to those special times, things, places, and feelings.

I remember the sagging mattress of my bed in the early morning, the bright homemade quilts that kept me warm, the homemade goosedown pillows, thick and fluffy under my head. I remember the sun streaming in through the east window of my room.

I would crawl from under the covers on a cold winter morning to reach for my clothes, and dress quickly: wool stockings, corduroy pants, and flannel shirts. I remember running down the creaky, wooden steps to a breakfast of hot oatmeal and warm, fresh bread spread with tart chokecherry jelly.

After pulling on a wool tassel cap with never a care about combing my thick, unruly hair, I got into my hand-me-down oversized coat, wool mittens, and red snowboots for the walk to school. I remember that walk as a special time in which to dream dreams of times, things, places, feelings.

Sometimes I read a book on this walk to school. My love of books, inherited from my mother, took me into other worlds. I remember reading *Little Women*, *Little Men*, *Little House on the Prairie*, *Little House in the Big Woods*. I discovered *Moby Dick* in the big ocean, *Lassie* in Alaska, and *So Big* by Edna Ferber. I read *Peggy Covers the News*.

I remember reaching the one-room schoolhouse — smoke streaming from the red brick chimney into the clouds. I would hang my coat on my special hook in the cloakroom. (How did we ever get a sophisticated word like "cloakroom" for a dirty entrance hall where our coats were kept?)

My desk had a hole where the inkwell should have been. I remember the penetrating smell and intermittent crackles of wood burning in the stove at the front of the room.

I remember hearing my teacher say, "Will the fifth grade please come up to the bench?" I remember many of the lessons taught to us as we sat on that bench at the front of the room. My favorite lessons were about history. I couldn't find out enough about the world I lived in and the people who lived there with me.

We went through our lessons, one grade after the other, sometimes helping the "slow readers" in the cloakroom. At lunch, we ate cold jelly sandwiches out of shiny syrup pails. Sometimes we traded foods.

Then came the hustle and bustle of getting into our "outside" clothes again for the long walk home. I remember sometimes running home — a mile in fifteen minutes. Sometimes I took a shortcut through our big woods. Sometimes I lost my way and needed to look to the sun for directions.

I remember coming into sight of my home — the welcome look of it when the sun shone on the front door. I remember the exhilarated feeling when I opened the door and my dog jumped from under the table to greet me; his rough, red tongue licking my cold, red face.

I would run up the stairs, jump over the banister, push open my bedroom door, and fall into the lumpy, unmade bed to rest and dream a little.

Then, I would change clothes and go downstairs to read the "funnies" on our kitchen table, and sneak cookies from the hidden place in the corner cabinet.

Putting on my tattered old jacket, I headed outside to do my farm chores. I remember the quick, lively mice that scurried in every direction when I pushed open the door to the feed shed, nearly tripping me as I dashed after them.

I remember carrying two five-gallon pails of ground feed from the shed to the chicken barn — they were heavy and clumsy, but I got done faster by taking two at a time! When I opened the chicken house door, the moist, musty, humid air of it engulfed me as I stepped inside. I remember the smell of pungent chicken manure, fresh straw, damp feathers and dry feed, the chickens clamoring around my feet, and the dust from pails of feed as I dumped them into the long metal wire feeders. I got out as soon as I could, back into the fresh air.

I remember going into the dairy barn to play with the baby kittens lying in their nests, all intertwined in deep sleep. I could never tell how many there were — they were just one mass of gray, yellow, white, and black bodies with tiny whiskers and twitches.

I remember the warm breath of the cows. When I fed them, they tried to bully me because I teased them. I always won because they were tied up and I was free! I remember the keen, intense cold of the haymow when I went up there to throw down hay for the cattle.

Then, I came back into the house to smells and sizzling sounds of pork chops frying, potatoes cooking, and bread baking. I remember the acrid smell that my wet clothes gave off after I hung them in front of the stove to dry.

I remember the cozy corner in the living room where I sat to do my homework and read, until I was ready for sleep again.

I remember crawling back into my snug bed and dreaming of times, things, places, and feelings.

A Tribute to Grandpa

by Michael Peters

Sharon and Walworth Townships, near Sharon,
Wisconsin, 1911-present

"If that's a chair, yer building it wrong." Grandpa smiled, at once happy to see me doing something constructive, but amused that it was not turning out. "Ya gotta make the back legs and backrest from one board, so it's all one piece. That way ya get a lot more strength out of it."

It was a June morning in 1956, one of those perfectly quiescent days in the country, the stillness only broken by the drone of an unseen airplane. My father was in the field cutting hay and my mother was tending the garden. I was a busy eight-year-old attempting to build a chair from some scrap lumber.

Walter Peters, my grandfather, had just arrived at the farm in his black 1950 Plymouth Deluxe four-door sedan. He limped over to where I was working. In the gathering morning heat, I could see the long sleeves of woolen underwear under his shirt. Grandpa never seemed to sweat any more than the rest of us, even on the hottest summer days.

The meaning of what he had just said about my chair

came to me in a rush. "Oh!" I exclaimed, "I get it now, Grandpa. Thanks." He and I worked together for the next hour building a sturdy chair with the backrest and back legs as an integral whole. Grandpa was kind to me, always taking an interest in what I was doing and helping out if he could.

One of Grandpa's legs was bent into a tortured bow, and he limped so badly that it was painful to watch him walk. I always had wondered if he was born that way. As we were working on the chair I asked, "Grandpa, was your leg always crooked like that?"

His face took on a certain sadness, and he said, "No. It happened in 1911, two years after me and yer grandma was married. I was cuttin' trees with my brother-in-law John Voss over north of Walworth. I was on one end of a two-man crosscut, sawing away on a big oak. When it fell, it bounced off another tree and kicked back straight at me.

"It pinned me down and broke my leg real bad. John got me out from under the tree and hauled me home in the wagon. He made a splint from two boards nailed together to make a trough. Your grandma and my two nieces, Gladys and Margaret, nursed me as I laid with my leg in that trough for four months, waitin' for it to knit. It didn't heal too straight, but I've always got along with it just the same."

Thus began the career of my grandfather. Despite his

crooked leg and severe limp, Grandpa Peters worked and farmed for the next fifty years in the Walworth, Wisconsin, area adjacent to the Illinois state line. In those days, farm life revolved around work horses.

Grandpa never liked tractors, preferring the company of horses instead. Tractors were powerful, but too inanimate and predictable for him to ever enjoy working with. A horse could be a friend. A tractor could not. Grandpa used to say, "You can love a horse, and it will love you back if you have good horse sense."

My father said that Grandpa would talk to his horses, a pair of chestnut Percherons named Tom and Jerry, as they worked together in the fields. With the sound of his voice or the click of his tongue, he was able to guide them, softly chanting, "Gee, haw, giddyup, whoa."

This special relationship between Grandpa and his horses involved a certain trust that never could be duplicated by a noisy, greasy tractor. Grandpa preferred the quiet meditative way of farming with horses. He felt that the obnoxious roar of a tractor disconnected him from Nature, obliterating the soft whisper of the wind in the tall grass, the gentle melodies of the summer songbirds, and most importantly, Grandma's voice calling him in for dinner.

His many years of farming with horses were happy years, and so Grandpa saw no reason to ever change. But new ways of doing things were in the air for farmers, and change was inevitable.

Grandpa never did farm with tractors and retired in 1942 to Harvard, Illinois, just south of the Wisconsin state line, and my parents took over the farm as Grandpa's tenants. For the next 20 years, he would drive out to the farm three to four times a week to do various odd jobs around the farm. He and my father were usually kept busy doing repair and construction work like fixing windows and doors, siding the house, or building a garage.

When there was no carpenter work to be done, Grandpa would sharpen his long scythe with a whetstone and cut weeds around the buildings. In all of the time I was growing up, I never once saw Grandpa drive a tractor. He would drive a car, but never a tractor.

Tractors were becoming common in the 1940s, displacing horses as the main source of power on the farm. My father, Donald Peters, never experienced the same joy of working with horses as did Grandpa. In 1946, he purchased a brand-new Oliver "70" tractor, three-bottom plow, and two-row mounted cultivator. The tractor was painted bright green. And as a boy, I would ride with Dad, standing on the drawbar, while clinging to a piece of clothesline tied to the rear fender.

The work horses were used less and less. Dad cut the long horse-hitches off the rest of the horse-drawn machinery and pulled everything with the new tractor. As a four-year-old, my only memories of Tom and Jerry were watching them nibbling their hay in their big wooden mangers, and leading them by their bridles to the tank in the barn for water.

My father sold the horses in 1952. It must have been difficult for Grandpa to say good-bye to his beloved horses. For some people this may have been cause for celebration, but for others it was not.

By this time, horses were merely anachronisms from a bygone era — doomed to slaughter in the name of progress, to a fate dictated by efficiency and economies of scale. The anticipation and excitement surrounding the arrival of this new age of agriculture was sharply contrasted by the antipathy and sadness of old-timers like Grandpa — as they said their final farewells to the way of farming they had known all their lives.

Today, the old wooden harness pegs still protrude from the wall of the "horse barn" (the part of the barn once partitioned off for the workhorses). The heavy leather harness is long absent. The old plank floor has been replaced with concrete. Dairy cows now stand where horses once stood.

Both my grandfather and father have passed away; the family farm entrusted to another generation. Now my children and I carry on the farming work of our ancestors. Only the harness pegs remain as a tribute to days gone by, my last physical link with Grandpa and a farming tradition which has disappeared into the wake of progress.

Walking in Faith

by Janet M. Price

Hardin County, near New Providence, Iowa, 1851-1852

I only knew him as Uncle William. That's because this story has been handed down four generations. The year was 1851.

Slowly, the ox-drawn covered wagons made their way across the 1200 miles of rough terrain from Surry (now Yadkin County), North Carolina, to the fertile prairies of central Iowa. The Reece brothers, William and Levi, and their families were among the forty-four determined pioneers who were seeking a place of new beginnings, away from the unrest in the south over issues of slavery.

Upon entering the southern part of Hardin County, Iowa, this small company decided to establish their community beside an unnamed, gentle creek that later became known as Honey Creek.

Although weary from the strenuous journey, they quickly began to fell the plentiful oak and walnut trees. A well-bonded group ranging in ages from eight weeks to grandparents in their seventies, they worked together feverishly day in and day out. It took hard, physical work to build their log houses using simple tools, almost primitive in nature.

Cold winter winds soon began to blow and it became a daily task to scoop out the snow that sifted in through the cracks. Although optimistic for a better life here, that first year led some to become homesick and disheartened. Springtime, however, brought new hope and they became encouraged to stay as they saw the community grow.

Sometime later, it was discovered that the land Uncle William had selected was not accurately numbered. Hearing of William's plight, a newcomer to the area decided that he wanted that prime land for his own. This stranger promptly set out on horseback to ride the sixty miles to Des Moines.

Now this group of staunch Quakers had faithfully met together for morning meeting. Uncle William had never neglected attending services and today would be no exception. Immediately after the meeting, William set out on foot to face this personal battle, armed with the prayers of family and friends. He walked all day on a path that was nearly non-existent in places and into the darkness of the night.

Knowing William had no horse, the stranger stopped for a night's rest, confident he would have no trouble securing the property he intended to claim from another. Beginning again early the next morning he arrived at the State building promptly at nine o'clock. He swung off his horse and gingerly started up the steps.

To his utter amazement, the door suddenly opened

and out stepped Uncle William. Finding the office door open a few minutes earlier, William had quickly completed the paper that legally made the land his.

Now, nearly 150 years later, the richness of the land continues to provide its bounty. Pictures remind us of those dear loved ones. Yet the true heritage they left us wasn't the material goods to be hoarded away, but the inner strength they received from a faith in God and trusting Him to daily meet their needs.

From generation to generation, this legacy is now handed down to us who would seek and then walk in the faith.

Snowstorms and Prairie Fires

by Muriel Ferris

Audubon and Elmwood Townships, Clay County, near Downer, Minnesota, 1890s

My Grandma was born in Scotland in 1871. In 1872, when she was just a year old, she came with her father, mother, sister, and two brothers to the United States. They arrived in Duluth by boat, having sailed up the St. Lawrence River and through the Great Lakes. From Duluth, they came to Audubon, Minnesota, and settled there. They lived in the woods in a tar-paper shanty with a sod roof. Sometimes when it rained, the water would come right through. Then it was time to put on a new sod roof.

There were lots of berries in the woods and Grandma and her brothers and sisters liked to pick them. They also helped their parents tap the trees and make maple syrup. There were Indians in the woods. They were friendly Indians, but the children were a little afraid when they would hear them in the woods or along the water's edge.

When Grandma was quite young, her mother died, and after that she lived with her grandma. Later they came to Downer to live, walking all the way from Audubon (about 25 miles) and bringing their herd of about 20 cattle with them. Her grandma led one cow while she walked behind it, her brothers walking behind the herd to keep them in line. They camped overnight on the way there, starting out again the next morning.

The land around Downer was all prairie, with tar-paper shanties scattered all over. There were no good roads, just "prairie roads," which were wagon trails across the prairie. They put up many stacks of hay that summer, but a prairie fire, not uncommon in those days, swept across the hot, dry hayland, burning everything in its way. There would be no feed for the winter, so they took their cows and went back to Audubon.

The following spring they came back to Downer, this time in a covered wagon, and with horses instead of oxen. Here they lived in a tar-paper shanty.

They burned wood in their old-fashioned cookstove, which was kept red-hot most of the time. The winters were cold and the storms were terrific. On one occasion, her dad went for a load of wood, and when he returned home, the snow was piled all around the shanty, and he could not get in the door. Grandma and the others inside opened the window and pulled the snow inside, into washtubs, so he could crawl in through the window. He and the boys then took shovels and cleared away the snow from the door, which opened to the inside instead of to the outside as ours do now. This was done because it was impossible to push the door outward after a snowstorm. The father of one family had to remove part of the sod roof to get into

130

his house after a snowstorm.

Grandma grew to womanhood in Downer, and in 1891 was married to Walter Cook, Jr. He and his father built a new two-story house. There was one room on each floor and there they settled down.

Prairie fires were common in those days and the early settlers were always on the lookout for that dreaded enemy. One day when Grandpa Cook and his dad were gone to town in their wagon, a prairie fire started. It started from sparks from a train. It was heading straight for Grandpa's farm, burning everything as it came along. Great-grandma and Grandma hurried to put out the fire.

Grandma had to take her baby girl, Cora (my mother), along as there was no one to leave her with, pushing the baby carriage along as fast as she could. My Grandma and Great-grandma each had a gunny sack and fought the flames as best as they could, beating them down with their sacks.

It was a hard fight and they were very tired and glad indeed when help came. They finally succeeded in halting the fire before it reached the buildings, but not before it had burned the entire west half of their section, which included many stacks of hay.

They were very thankful it did not take their home.

The Cellar

by Donald C. Rupert

Fairfield Township, near Columbiana, Ohio, 1915-1930

Our 1850 farmhouse had a cellar. It was a "proper" cellar, common to our area in my boyhood in the 1920s. The uneven dirt floor was sufficiently damp to never become dusty. It was unheated but snug enough that nothing froze.

My youthful memories of our cellar resolve around two characteristics: it was dark, and it smelled. The darkness was only a little fearsome. The odors were mostly non-threatening and some even inviting.

The old dark walls were flat rough stones, about one inch thick, laid up without mortar. Detritus from the decaying rock and soil trickling through the open rock layers filled the ledges and sifted down to the dirt floor. That part of the wall above ground was made of massive cut sandstone blocks. The low ceiling was raw rough-sawn oak, colored by time to a very dark brown. No whitewash was ever used on the walls or ceiling.

Standing around on the black dirt floor were several large black iron kettles and some old unpainted rough wooden tables and benches. Two small windows in the east wall did little to diminish the prevailing gloom. No amount of cleaning ever overcame an air of untidiness that the dimness both partially hid and accentuated.

In spite of the darkness of the cellar, it was never a forbidding place to me. One reason may have been the cookie crock which was an earthen three-gallon container where moist cookies were stored. Mother's request to "fetch" something from "down cellar" usually received a willing response especially when the cookie crock was on duty. It was a challenge to get some cookies without the noisy lid betraying your actions.

As I entered the cellar, my eyes gradually adjusted to the dimness and, as the gloom receded, the smells became more assertive and revealing. These varied from season to season both in presence and dominance. Some disappeared completely, some lingered faintly, and a few were readily detected at any time.

I recall the mild earthy odor from the potato bin in the darkest corner behind the cellar steps. The fragrance from the apples nearby was more inviting. Crates filled with Romes, Baldwins, Grimes, Spies, and Kings, each with a distinctive flavor and aroma, blended to produce an exciting and enticing bait for a hungry boy. The spicy smell from the vinegar barrel was present all year. Shelves on the south wall were loaded with Mother's canned meats, fruits, and vegetables.

Mother canned and canned and canned. The meats included pork tenderloins, smoked sausages, and head cheese made from pork head-meats and liver. This made a rich topping for pancakes or was combined with corn-meal mush to produce scrapple. All of these had a layer of lard on top.

The fruits included strawberries, sweet cherries, sour cherries, blackberries, grapes, peaches, pears, plums, and pickled Sweet Bow apples. The canned vegetables were peas, green beans, yellow beans, lima beans, sweet corn, beets, carrots, tomatoes, tomato juice, pickles, pickled green tomatoes, and pickled peppers.

Jars of jam, jellies and preserves, plus "end-of-the-garden" relish or mixed pickle completed the cornucopia. In June and July, the early morning sun shone on these shelves to expose the only attractive view in the cellar. No odors there, but the sauerkraut crock nearby added its aroma.

The most memorable odor and one that persisted throughout the year came from our butchering process. The hams, shoulders, and bacon sides were spread on tables along the east wall where cold air, entering from the outside cellar door, cooled them. They were rubbed with salt, some saltpeter, and brown sugar daily until Grandpa Rupert said they were "done."

This meat was smoked for a few days over a slow-burning fire of apple and hickory wood in our smokehouse, a small shed for smoking and storing meats. One March day, high winds blew sparks from the fire, destroying the building and most of the meat. After that, "liquid smoke" replaced the natural smoke. This commercial product was brushed on the meat as it lay on the curing tables to give us the "smoked" flavor. Curing completed, the meat, wrapped in muslin cloth, was stored in the granary. Though the meat was gone, the curing tables in the cellar retained the strong smoky odor. We butchered in November and again in March, reinforcing the odor.

There were odors of decay also. The stench of rotting potatoes could be overwhelming. It was, and is, the worst vegetative odor with which I am familiar. At first hint of this in the waning days of winter, my brother and I sorted them and also removed the sprouts from the remaining good ones. Some apples decayed also, but this aroma is milder.

When we had an excess of apples, there was a mushy mass of rotting apples to remove in the spring. The long-est-keeping apple we had was the Rome Beauty. It was an attractive dark-red, solid apple that was tasteless com-pared to our favorites. Its only redeeming feature, besides being good for pies, was that it was still there when our favorites were gone.

At the north end of the cellar, four stone steps led up between rough shaped stone walls to provide access to the outdoors. The old weathered door at the bottom of the steps could be closed tightly and securely with some ef-fort. It was left open from May into the chilly nights of fall, and only aromas from the vinegar barrel and the "liquid smoke" on the curing tables outlasted the fresh air of summer. Fortunately for us, a skunk, seen wandering in through the open door, wandered out again without making his tell-tale contribution to the atmosphere!

Today the old cellar is gone. It is a basement now with a cement floor, electric lights, a hot-water boiler with attendant fuel tanks, and gleaming white electrical appliances. Our butchering process ended with the advent of the local locker freezer plants with adjoining slaughter facilities. The vinegar barrel disappeared as did the sauerkraut crock. Some became antique displays along with the big butchering kettles. Heat from the boiler made impractical the storage of apples and potatoes. All the old smells are gone, replaced by the modern stink of fuel oil.

Cellars, like ours, were common until World War II. Some were blessed with cold spring water providing a place to keep butter, cheese, and milk. Our spring-house was nearby, downhill from the outside cellar door. These cellars and spring-houses were an essential part of the self-sufficient farm life that became passe with the coming of good roads, the automobile, electricity, and modern distribution systems.

Today's supermarkets have made self-sufficient farms a rarity.

The Joys of Indiana Bible School

by Pat Furber

Marshall County, near Plymouth, Indiana, 1940s

"Next Wednesday, we'll go clean North Salem for Bible School," Mom would announce in early June. School was out, and Bible School was the highlight of the summer. Now, our Bible School of the 1940s was not like the vacation Bible schools of today. We didn't just run over to the church for a couple of hours each morning. Ours was a total commitment; we lived there for ten days.

Bible School was held at North Salem, Indiana, in a little country church about seventeen miles from our home. People came from all over Indiana every June to study the Bible, conduct church business, and just enjoy being with friends. We chose North Salem because it had a sleeping dormitory that would accommodate most of us.

The dormitory stood silent and empty during the winter except for the families of mice and spiders who made it their winter home. In early June, those of us who lived nearby went down to clean the spider-webby place. We prayed for a nice day, then aired all the comforters and straw tick mattresses. While they were blowing in the breeze, we mopped cement floors and showers.

Then we tackled the kitchen and dining area, which

was in the basement of the church. The church was built like a bi-level, with a half a dozen steps leading up to the chapel, and the same amount of steps going down to the kitchen. Here were three long trestle tables with benches. A pass-through partially hid the kitchen beyond, which housed gas stoves and a big work table, an ice box, a sink with a pump, and of course, the dishes.

Our work was cut out for us. My cousin Donna and I were assigned to wash all the dishes. Then we scrubbed the tables and benches. By this time, the gnawing pains in our tummies and the other workers' arrival with their potluck lunch signaled a welcome break.

Many of the same people helped clean every year, so we could count on Sister Heyde to bring deviled eggs, Sister Zekiel's banana pudding with peanuts on top, and Grandma's doughnuts.

A week later, we would all return to our cleaned quarters. Since Donna and I had done the cleaning of the beds, we felt justified in reserving our corner bed in the dormitory that had a real mattress instead of a straw tick. Also, we took advantage of our little corner by nailing up a blanket for our private dressing room. Cross-ventilation was another blessing we enjoyed in our corner bed. Those June nights were really hot and humid!

The boys and older men were below us. Most of the husbands and fathers were just evening and weekend attenders, and seldom slept there. A few young families with babies were housed in other rooms downstairs. Their privacy was limited, however, as we had to traipse through their rooms to the shower.

Of course there were privies out in the yard behind the church. We girls were mortified to visit these small buildings, as we had to walk past the boys' dorm and they were always outside, shooting baskets.

Bill Warner, a plumber who was married to a relative of ours in Bremen, built in a bathroom on our top floor. At first, we were ecstatic. But it never functioned past the first day. Every year we would have high hopes for its success, but it always let us down and we were destined to walk with red faces past the smirking boys.

Sometimes our open windows were not an asset. I mentioned the "older" men who slept downstairs. My grandad was one of them. He looked forward to visiting with his friend, Bill Huffer, each year. Bill was from southern Indiana so this was their one chance to catch up on crops and politics. They slept in the dormitory but they kept "farmers' hours." Out of courtesy to their young sleeping companions, they would head to the bench by the side of the church every morning about 5:30. Here they discussed everything from whether to plant corn or beans that year to whether FDR should run a third term. Both Bill and Grandad were getting quite deaf, so we with the open window were treated to every word of these early morning discussions.

This woke us up for breakfast, though. Grandma was our "chief cook" so we could generally anticipate delicious meals. But breakfast was an exception. Grandma was on a very limited budget. Breakfast consisted of puffed rice, bread, oleo (the kind that had to have the coloring added), apple butter, hominy, milk, and coffee.

I refused to touch the oleo because it looked like lard before it was colored. I just settled for a piece of bread slathered with apple butter, and sneaked away before my mother could see how little I'd eaten.

We welcomed Bible School as the opportunity to see our church friends from all over the state. There were Shirley and Bonnie from southern Indiana, Betty Dick, whose dad was a minister, Jeanette from Hartford City, Betty and Barbara from Illinois whose aunt lived near the church, and others that lived close by. We chewed on suckers and giggled over our current "crushes."

Friendships were our main motivation for coming to Bible School, but our adult leaders had more lofty reasons for our attending. We were there to study the Bible and we had three Bible classes each day. We studied everything from the measurements of the Jewish tabernacle to the various parts of the "whole armour of God" (Ephesians 6:11-17).

We became really close to many of the ministers. If we worked hard, they took us swimming to the nearby Lake of the Woods, and later baptized us in the same lake. They were our friends as well as our teachers.

Of course we had other mundane duties, such as cleaning tables, sweeping floors, washing the leaf lettuce donated by farm wives, and ringing the bell for meals. Sometimes we were given the coveted assignment of scouring the woods for ripe, wild strawberries. Grandma had plans for strawberry shortcake, but she was lucky if any got as far as the kitchen!

Our surroundings were humble compared to the sophisticated church conferences of today. But living accommodations were unimportant to us. The deep-rooted friendships we formed at the Indiana Bible School, the good people who nurtured us and taught us, were a basis of my faith and joy in living today.

Walking Beans

by Lois A. Schmidt

Kintire Township, near Belview, Minnesota, 1957-1970s

When we got married in October, 1946, soybeans as a farm crop were just beginning to gain a foothold. They usually were raised in a corn, wheat, or oats and beans rotation. After a few years, it developed into just a corn and beans rotation. Those were days of no chemical sprays for beans!

Cultivating was usually done three times, and that took care of a lot of weeds. But the weeds that were smart enough to grow in the row just forged right on ahead. And so — the weeds grew, and grew, and grew. Would that some people have the fortitude that weeds have!

Until one day in 1957. After my husband Floyd had finished cultivating the approximately 80 acres of beans, he came in the house and said, "Are you going to help me pull weeds out of those beans?" They were about 6 to 8 inches tall, at the time. I didn't exactly jump for joy at the thought!

Well, Faye, our oldest child, was nine. Vicki was seven. Alan was four, and Linda was only three years old. And, on a hot, hot day in June, we took a water jug and headed down to the field. Floyd was on one flank of our little group, taking two rows. Faye and Vicki each took one row apiece, and Alan and Linda were to do one row together, with me on the far side, doing two rows. That made a total of seven rows. Do you know how many rows of beans there are in an 80-acre field (which was half a mile long)?

We started out walking and pulling. Bend ... pull ... walk ... bend ...pull. A nine and a seven-year-old don't really value the results of doing away with weeds much, let alone a four and three-year-old! I wasn't too sure about it, myself!

We weren't out there very long before we excused the two youngest to play at the end; (even that gets boring when you have to do it for hours at a time). And it did take at least two hours to make it across 160 rods and back ... bend ... pull ... bend ... pull.

But, a couple years later, Alan and Linda joined us to make up our "team" of six, and in time, we each took three rows, so we covered a lot of ground each day.

We always went out very early in the morning, so it would be a bit cooler. But some nights, you know, don't cool down. And that really made the feet weight a ton apiece. In the afternoons, it was catch up with house and garden, while Floyd cultivated fields.

Some time later, we decided to try using a hoe. What a joy, not to have to bend ... in the heat. But of course, you often managed to take out some beans along with the weeds. So we had to be careful.

Cocklebur was a special menace, because it has such large leaves, cutting off the sun from the beans ... and of course the cocklebur grew the fastest. Except for the later ones, which hid under the beans, until you were past that row, and then they shot for the sky. Sometimes we went over a field twice! Not often, though.

Cocklebur seeds are quite large (up to one-half-inch), very prickly, and they float. In the past, when the cocklebur had gone to seed in some spots, the seeds floated into and around the lower, wet spots in the field — and grew thick as the hair on a dog. When sun and rain are favorable, beans grown like crazy, and so it was that before we got to some fields, the beans were quite tall. But the weeds were taller!

In the earlier years, (before we got them pretty well under control), after we had pulled out the cocklebur, the beans could hardly stay upright. In those kinds of spots, we still pulled the weeds, rather than hoe.

I remember one year when we got a lot of rain, and the fields were a sea of mud, but the weeds kept growing, so we had to walk in the mud. We ended up taking off our shoes, with mud up to our knees.

After a few years of so much special attention, we were gratified to see that we indeed did have beautiful bean fields — almost free of weeds. Even the thistles were giving up to the hoe. But then one day, when we were "walking beans" alongside our township road, a neighbor came

144

past, stopped and said, "Say, you missed a weed back there." And that was a neighbor whose bean fields had weeds — lots of them!

Funny that I can't recall the conversations that we had, but it seemed there was a lot of talking.

Faye always took it upon herself to figure out how many acres we had done so far ... anything for diversion!

And Vicki would stay with us most of the way across the fields, but going back was another story. She literally flew across the field. She did a good job, but I still have not figured out how she got her row done so quickly ... so she could get back to play with Alan and Linda.

And when the very last row was done, we always gave a "Hip, hip, hooray!" And I seem to remember feeling that maybe, just maybe, we'd make it through another hot summer — once the beans were done.

Looking back, I think it really was all for the best, although you might not have convinced me of it then. I think our kids learned a real good work ethic. All of them learned to work hard and what it is to feel proud of their work.

Anyway, I like to think that. They all turned out to be good workers, and I am so proud of them.

A Pig's Trip to Market
by Alvin Wiechman

near Buffalo Lake, Minnesota, 1982

One day in the spring of 1982, I loaded a huge sow into my pickup, covered with a wooden box. It had heavy wooden sides, a plywood cover on top, and hardwood stakes that fit into the pockets of the pickup box.

Well, I had started for Buffalo Lake, Minnesota, to where Muller's hog-buying station was located.

As I headed into a strong northwest wind, it pulled pretty hard, so I stepped on the gas to make better headway. With about two and a half or three miles to go yet, I noticed the box begin to lift up, ever so slowly. The wind got under it and lifted the box so nice and gentle, landing it in the ditch.

It dawned on me right away, I couldn't stop or the big old sow would jump out. No way was I going to let her do that.

In the rear view mirror I saw her going for the back to jump out while we were going about 40 miles an hour. To keep her from going out the back I hit the brakes, slamming her into the cab behind me. She got back on her feet again and then looked over the right side to jump out there, so I quickly turned the steering wheel, throwing her back

146

to the middle of the pickup box.

After doing this a few times she finally settled down and stood still, looking straight ahead over the top of the cab, nose into the wind. I noticed a peculiar effect on the drivers I met coming toward me. Most had eyeballs big as tea cups. Some cars pulled over and stopped. One lady of about middle age, I guess, had a look on her like she was seeing a ghost.

When we got to Muller's hog-buying station, I drove by the window where the buyer was. He looked out the window with a look of amazement and disbelief.

I had to hurry and back up to the unloading chute, 'cause the old sow wanted off of there right now. When the buyer came around the corner, he asked me how in the heck could I haul a big sow that way.

I made-believe that it was no big deal. As I told him, I hauled all my tame pigs that way.

I'm not sure if he believed me or not. To this day he still talks about that episode in wonderment.

Kids on the Farm

by Faye M. Molander

Lincoln County, near Vesper, Kansas, 1930s

"Let's play house!" With that suggestion my sister Lola Mae and I went out the door. As the screen door closed, we ran down the porch steps into our backyard shaded by a giant spreading elm tree.

It was a lazy summer day, and our playhouse was outlined by various lengths of scrap lumber and bricks. It had two rooms with one door and was sparsely furnished with a small iron stove, a bucket full of sand, and a wooden box for a cupboard holding our tin dishes, a rolling pin, and a few old spoons. Sometimes when Mother wasn't using her small wooden table to hold the tub of cold rinse water on wash days, we could use the table in the playhouse.

"Make believe" was what made the experience challenging. Our foods came from the farmyard. Brown beans came from the locust tree seed-pods. Peas were the small round green seeds from a plant that produced a pod to be popped after the flower had bloomed. We called it a popweed, lacking a better known name. There were plenty of greens for salads. We also made mud pies and ate mulberries in season.

But our more delectable sweets were cookies that were patterned after the newly-marketed, store-bought domed marshmallow cookies covered with thin chocolate icing. I made up a recipe for those cookies! I don't remember the measurements, but the ingredients were dirt, sand, and water from the nearby pump under the windmill. They were formed in a toy gravy ladle and dipped in a white powder we found in small deposits in the banks of a gravel pit in our pasture. A plate of these beautiful cookies provided the goodies for a lovely tea party.

Our farm was the first one bordering a small Kansas village. We walked a quarter mile to school and a mile into the village to play with friends. Our cousins were frequent playmates. From time to time we would visit "make believe" friends who lived in various places around the farmyard. Maybelle lived under a locust tree between the red brooder house and Butler granary. Another friend lived under a mulberry tree next to a small tool shed.

Although we played with dolls, it was more fun to play with our cats! Farm cats lived in the barn and were fed warm milk as soon as the hand-operated separator extracted the cream from the milk. The cats crowded around our feet as we poured milk into a pan near the stone separator house. They were good mousers, too. We had a green wicker doll buggy and often tried to give the cats a ride. They didn't stay in the buggy very long before they jumped out. But we kept trying!

We loved the cats and felt sorry for them in the cold weather when snow was on the ground. Once, we decided to sew some boots for their paws, but they didn't appreciate our concern and worked them off using their mouth and paws.

The lazy days of summer came to a sudden halt when wheat harvest time arrived. My sister and I always shared farm chores, but those days brought more responsibilities. We helped prepare vegetables from the garden and cook the meals. We listened carefully as the conversations revealed each day's progress and how much each field yielded per acre. We carried water to the chickens, kept the oyster-shell feeder full, scattered wheat on the ground for them each evening, and gathered the eggs from the nests in the chicken house.

I learned how to milk our cow, Pet, in the evenings after she entered her stall in the barn. We usually had a calf staked on a chain in the outer yard to eat grass, and we carried several buckets of water to it every day. One summer, Lola Mae and I sold our calf at the end of the season and were excited to have the money to purchase our first bicycle.

Mother said we had "running water" because Lola Mae carried buckets of water from the pump into the house. I carried wood for our cookstove in bushel baskets. The heating stove in the living room burned chunks of wood which I piled in neat rows on the back porch. Every fall,

Daddy cut trees from our grove of cottonwoods and hand-sawed chunks of wood, stacking up four walls into a large woodpile, filled with the smaller pieces for the cookstove.

Most kids in the country in the 1930s grew up without electricity — but with imagination, persistence, and an understanding of what it takes in real life to "play house."

No, we weren't poor; we were rich with a loving family, a comfortable home, and plenty of food produced on the farm. Happy childhood memories are a blessing for which I am thankful.

Saturday Night in the Summer Time

by Lloyd Mather

near Sidney, Iowa, 1944-1945

Saturday night in the summer is really something special! During the school year, when you have your friends around you on a daily basis, Saturday night isn't that big a deal. But in the summer time, Saturday night takes on an entirely different atmosphere.

About mid-week, or at least by Thursday, we would start making the big plans for the trip into town on Saturday night. Living out in the country seemed to inhibit our social life, not only by the distance involved but also by the work that seemed never to get done. But we never felt deprived of the fun things that the city kids were getting to do because we really didn't know what was going on in town anyway.

During the week, we knew we had field work to do, chores with the livestock, supper about six o'clock, listen to our favorite programs around the big Bendix radio, perhaps a few minutes late out on the big wrap-around porch, and then off to bed. We never did get accustomed to the five o'clock alarm the next morning, no matter how early we got to bed the night before.

152

But Saturday night was a treat! We could hardly keep our minds on the chores. More than once, we would have to go back and do something over because we got in a hurry or were daydreaming about something else and didn't do it right the first time. Mom and Dad had the ultimate threat on their side, "You can't go to town unless you've got your chores done!" Boy, would we scurry around like field mice, trying to get everything done right so we wouldn't be late getting into town.

We lived only a mile from town, so we boys would usually walk. We wanted to get there and meet our friends before the show started. Mom and Dad were more content to take their time. And of course, they always had to load the cream and the eggs in the truck before they could leave.

As we boys walked to town, we were full of talk and laughter. We were scrubbed as clean as the barrel shower outside could get us. With a short-sleeved shirt hanging outside a clean pair of blue jeans, we were ready for whatever the bright lights had to offer.

Dad would always give us our weekly allowance just before we were ready to leave for town with the usual admonishment, "Boys, you might try to save a bit of it for next week." But to young teenagers, next week was a month away, and there was plenty of time to save for that.

We most generally went to the picture show on Saturday night, because the folks didn't want us just walking the streets. Besides, the shows on Saturday night were always new — westerns, or the latest with Jimmy Stewart, or gangsters with James Cagney. We sat there, with the smell of popcorn nearby, giving side glances to the couples next to us whenever a light scene would come on the screen, hoping to catch some guy with his arm around his girl. We wouldn't spend our money on the popcorn because that was something we could have at home.

When the movie was over, we and our friends would hightail it over to the ice cream parlor. New in town, it was painted white and the electric ceiling fans kept the place cool. The best part was the different kinds of ice cream they kept in the cardboard barrels in the freezers behind the glass panels. Compared to the drug store, that only had four or five flavors, the ice cream parlor was a veritable gold mine. There were two or three different kinds of chocolate, about the same for vanilla, about three kinds of strawberry, and so ran the gamut of colors and flavors until you could hardly keep track of it all.

The best was the butter brickle! It had that golden cream color, with all of that heavenly butter brickle spread throughout. One huge scoop was a nickel, two scoops for a dime! We soon learned that the nickel scoop left us with a nickel that we could spend on a cherry Coke over at the drug store.

So we would sit, enjoying those delicious smells, feeling the cool of the ceiling fans down the back of our shirts and on our arms, and talk about things that are terribly important to teenagers.

Sometimes we wouldn't stop for the cherry Cokes at the drug store. The Ford garage had a Coke machine with ice water in it to cool the pop. The cold drinks included Coke, orange, 7-Up, strawberry, grape, lime, and two or three other flavors. We would put our nickel in the coin slot, open the lid, and have all those wonderful choices — from which we usually took the Coke. If we weren't careful, it would bubble up and sting our noses, and that was always a funny sensation.

Afterwards we would go off into twos, threes, or fours, walking the six-block rectangle around the big red brick court house. It was a lazy walk, hands in the pockets, a rock-kicking kind of a shuffle. Whenever we would pass some girls, we would all turn quiet, like we had something terribly important to talk about and we didn't want them in on it. In fact we wouldn't even speak to them because if one of us did, he was sure to get razzed by the others.

As the evening grew later, the people began to thin out on the sidewalks, and the sound of cars starting up replaced the hum of conversation on the street corners. Parents could be heard calling out their goodbyes, with "See you tomorrow in church," or, "See you next week."

The Ford garage turned off the big sign out in front and banged shut the overhead doors off Main Street. The creamery turned out the light in back, and you could hear the metallic click of the locked hasp.

We boys always found our folks in time to avoid the long walk back home. We would hunker down in the back of the truck, talking about the events of the evening. To hear us talk, we all had different tales of how we perceived the evening. Undoubtedly, it was a memorable evening that would be discussed until we started plans for next Saturday night.

As we pulled into the driveway, the headlights picked up Rex, the nondescript farm dog, a self-appointed greeting party of one, and the beady eyes of the grey short-haired cat sitting balled up on the back porch.

As the truck coughed into a dead silence, there was an eerie stillness about the farmstead, punctuated by the sound of the lids banging on the feeder down in the hog lot. Somewhere a calf bawled out in the dark of night for its mother and then all was quiet again.

Dad punched off the truck lights, turning everything pitch black. Around the corner of the house came the blue haze of the mercury vapor light. Rex came out and stretched himself up against the first body he came to, in a joyful reunion of family. "One of you boys grab the cream cans and bring them in, will you?" was the final reminder that another memorable Saturday night of the summer had come to an end.